# Memento Mori

## Classifying Nineteenth Century Ontario Gravestones

By Laura Suchan, M.A.

Revised and updated 2012

*For my Father*
*Detlef Paul Suchan*
*1941-2003*

All photographs by Laura Suchan unless otherwise stated.

ISBN 978-0-9916799-0-4

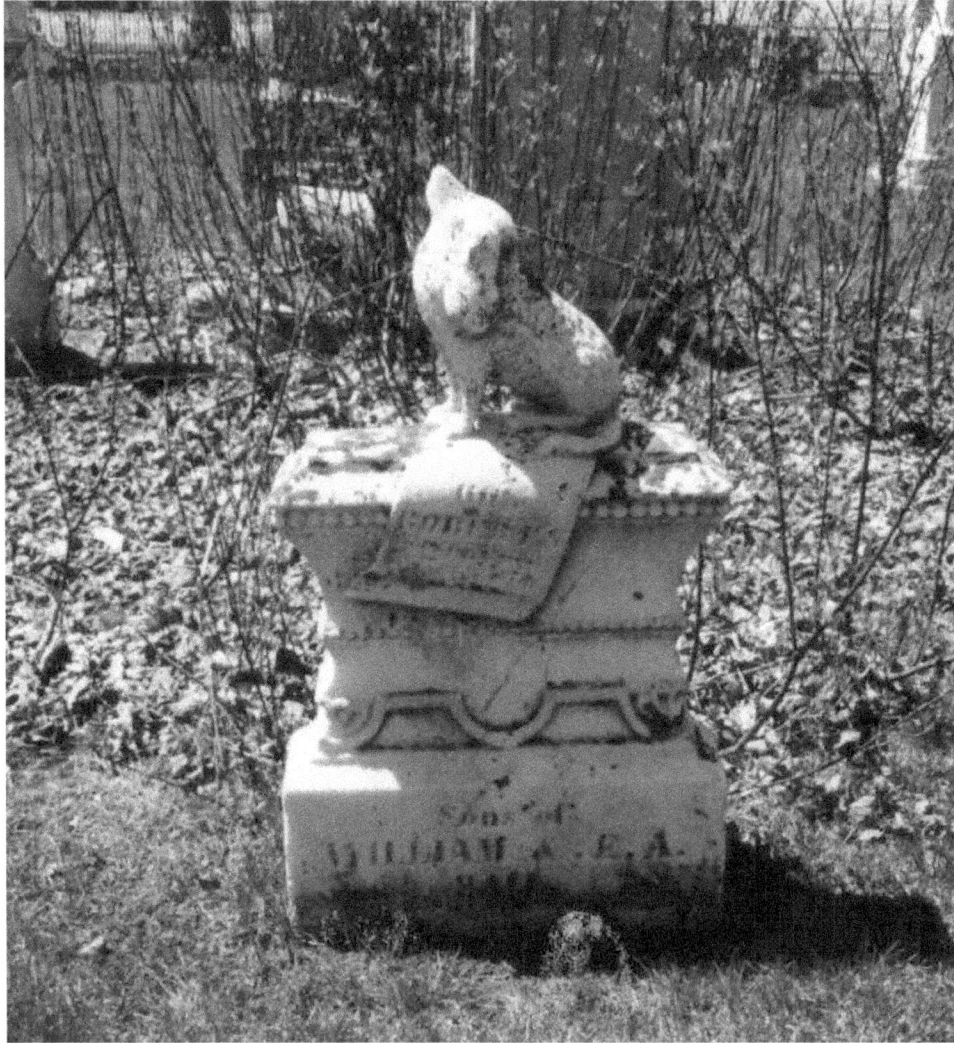

# INTRODUCTION

*Kind friends beware as you pass by*
*As you are so once was I*
*As I am you must be*
*Prepare therefore to follow me.*

~ Early Epitaph

*When Albert Henry's wife died of typhoid in 1866, she was buried in the Harbour Pioneer Cemetery on the hill near their home at the lakefront in Oshawa. It was a particularly sad time for the family as Harriet was only 23 years of age and left behind two young daughters. Her father-in-law, Reverend Thomas Henry, writes of the time, "On Monday we went down to Bowmanville and brought back her lifeless remains, and deposited them in their last resting place in the burying ground at Port Oshawa. How sad to see that blighted flower so early placed in the grave – only 23 years of age. Daughter, wife, mother, Christian – Farewell."* Harriet Guy Henry's remains continue to rest in the Harbour Pioneer Cemetery on Bonnie Brae point in Oshawa.

Memoirs of Thomas Henry, 1880

Venture down any back road in Ontario and before long you will come upon a historic graveyard. These graveyards have long been a part of our cultural landscapes and rural communities. Viewed in the nineteenth century as foul and unhygienic places, graveyards were usually situated in rural areas outside the town limits. Today these graveyards have much to teach us about not only a community's history but Victorian society in general. Early Ontario gravestones are windows into the past and besides providing the biographical data of the deceased, gravestones should also be viewed as a form of early artistic and cultural expression.

Unfortunately gravestones have received little attention from historical researchers, at least here in Canada. Information gained from the stones relating to birth and death dates, surnames and family relationships has a practical application to identify the deceased. Even the epitaphs, such as the example provided above, are often viewed in a whimsical way, as entertaining reading. As a result the iconography or pictorial imagery of the gravestones has largely been ignored as an expression of culture and an area worthy of study.

Besides functioning as a memorial to the deceased, gravestones should also be viewed as a form of expression capable of providing insight into several aspects of nineteenth century life. On the surface, the visual imagery of the symbolic representations or motifs , present on the stones functions as a decorative element, an early example of folk-art expression. Below the surface, however, there is a deeper, more symbolic, function to the motifs, one which parallels contemporary thoughts in religious philosophy and popular culture. As a medium of expression gravestones reaffirm the position of the deceased within the community and celebrate relationships. On an artistic level, gravestones offer insights into popular culture for they were chosen by, and for all, classes of society. Motifs were specifically chosen by the carver or family members to communicate messages about the departed and their significance. Motifs were also chosen to convey messages about religion or society which can be interpreted depending on the style and sometimes the time period. In an era when illiteracy was common, carvers relied on the symbols to convey messages of mortality and spirituality to those settlers unable to read verse. Themes relating to life, death and the hope for everlasting life are just some of the messages portrayed on the stones. Motifs held a practical function for the living as well as the dead.

# The Need for a Classification System

Gravestone iconography exhibits a remarkable progression of artistic ability, culture and religious expression throughout the nineteenth century. Unfortunately the study of gravestone motifs has been virtually ignored by genealogists and the local and provincial organizations undertaking the task of transcribing data from Ontario's early cemeteries. The emphasis has been placed on transcribing the biographical data and, in some cases, the epitaphs while ignoring for the most part, the motifs present on the gravestones. Part of the reluctance to record the motifs stems from the view they are merely a decorative adornment which, although attractive, does not further the study of Ontario history and is not therefore worthy of recording. Researchers have also expressed uncertainty as to how to deal with the sheer number of expressions embracing countless variations of form and treatments.

Time is of the essence for if the motif information is not recorded soon, it will be lost forever. In fact much of the information contained on the stones is in danger of being destroyed from the effects of vandals, harsh environmental agents, atmospheric pollution, weathering and incorrect repair and conservation techniques. Marble and limestone monuments erode with the effects of acid rain causing carvings to soften and the inscriptions to fade [1]. The surface of the marble stones can convert to gypsum in reaction with atmospheric pollution. Gypsum may also combine with carbon to form a harmful black crust which in time will crumble away resulting in the loss of the entire surface including carvings and inscriptions. This crust generally forms in areas of deep carvings such as willow trees [2].

On the human side of the problem is the damage caused by vandals. Nineteenth century stones are extremely brittle and if pushed over may easily break into fragments. The Ontario Cemeteries Act (Revised) 1990 does provide a small degree of protection by stating that any person who moves or damages a marker is liable to the cemetery owner for any damage. The Act also stipulates standards for the stabilizing and preservation of markers. The Ontario Heritage Act enables municipalities to designate heritage conservation districts providing some protection from demolition or alteration. Currently Ontario has over 120 cemeteries designated under the Act for historical or architectural value or interest. Unfortunately, at this time, no cemeteries in Oshawa are designated as such. [3]

With the gravestones facing countless dangers and daily threats, vital historical information is being lost. A sense of urgency is reflected in the fact transcription records prepared a mere twenty years ago for graveyards in Oshawa, Ontario contain information which is unavailable now in the cemeteries due to deterioration or theft of stones. Thus it is important that all organizations such as the Ontario Genealogical Society be persuaded to systematically record motifs along with the biographical information when transcribing stones.

Previous attempts by organizations to record and classify the motifs have failed because a standardized system for organizing the designs, based on the predominant element, is not available. A standardized categorization system would alleviate many of the concerns currently facing researchers in the field and ensure all elements are being duly recorded homogeneously to facilitate accurate comparisons and evaluations province wide. Canadian, and specifically Ontario, thanatological [4] research has lagged behind efforts in the United States to develop a standardized system of recording which provides for a common format for all data collected. Groups such as the Association for Gravestone Studies (AGS) in Massachusetts have been at the forefront in development of transcription methods.

Present systems in use in Ontario are generally site specific and too narrowly defined to allow for accurate comparisons to be made between cemeteries in different areas of the province. Until a standardized approach to recording gravestone motifs is in use, province wide, trends in design will be difficult to observe. I believe nineteenth century gravestone motifs can be organized into several manageable stylistic categories based on the predominate design which would allow for uniform recording practices. The goal is to develop a simple and practical system featuring generic categories which would be user friendly in a field situation. The classification system will then be applied to a standard graveyard inventory sheet providing an effective, new tool for studying early Ontario graveyards. Moreover it will be illustrated how many of the design expressions exhibit change over the course of the nineteenth century in relation to the prevailing societal trends embracing religion, thought and architecture.

Stones of Alex and Harriet Greig in Union Cemetery, Oshawa.
Photographed in 1996, the stones are easy to read and the motifs are
clear. Compare this photo with the one below.

Same stones, photo taken 10 years later. In the short span of 10 years
the stones have become very difficult to decipher. Photo by Melissa Cole.

# Background

*A monument is the last tribute of affection that the living can tender to commemorate the memory of the beloved dead.  How necessary then that it should be an embodiment of art and tasteful design.*

~ Industries of Canada, 1886

Prior to the nineteenth century large graveyards were not known. Settlers were either buried on family property or if a member of a church, in the church yard in order to be closer to God. Often viewed as "foul smelling, unattractive eyesores" and "harbingers of disease" [5] it is no wonder settlers began to look further afield for places to bury their dead as churchyards began to fill.  During the mid 1800's the rural cemetery movement, as defined by Jacob Bigelow of Boston,   developed over the concern that  cemeteries were  becoming  increasingly unhygienic and  overcrowded. These rural cemeteries, usually situated in areas outside of the town limits, were  not associated with a church.   Mount Auburn Cemetery in Cambridge Massachusetts is acknowledged to be the first rural cemetery in America.  Landscaping became an important feature of these cemeteries and part of their appeal. Hall and Bowden  believe  these cemeteries  are  more  aptly  described  as  "garden  cemeteries"  `as they often featured beautiful views.[6]  Catarqui Cemetery in Kingston was directly influenced by the rural and garden cemetery movement in the United states as well as by the design of Mount Auburn.  Catarqui's design incorporated ponds and waterways as well as the mature trees found at the site to produce an outstanding example of a rural cemetery design.

Following on the heels of the  rural cemetery movement in the  United  States,  a  park philosophy  soon  emerged  in cemetery design   supporting the replacement of gravestones by flat name plates to preserve the park like vistas.   Such graveyards were designed as places to be enjoyed as leisure spots  for  the  living  and  are  closely  related  to  the  city beautification movement taking place in the latter half of the nineteenth century. [7]  Park cemeteries would add another amenity to be enjoyed by residents at their leisure.   Although never fully adopted in its intended form, portions of Mount Pleasant Cemetery in Toronto do reflect several of the design elements specific to the park cemetery.  When the cemetery opened in 1876 there were more than 12 miles of carriage drives which would take visitors passed ponds and hills.  Today Mount Pleasant features walking trails, exceptional gardens, fountains and statues.   On  a  lesser  scale  would  have been the Harbour Pioneer cemetery in Oshawa which was surrounded by a ring of trees and overlooked the tranquil waters of Lake Ontario.

The  gravestones  in  early  cemeteries  were  used  to identify gravesites and provide a memorial  to  the  deceased. The Cemeteries Act defines  a  marker  as   "any  monument, tombstone, plaque, headstone, cornerstone, or other structure or ornament affixed to or intended to be affixed to a burial lot, mausoleum crypt, columbarium niche or other structure or place intended for the deposit of human remains".[8]  The very earliest grave markers were made of wood which was readily available and easy to carve but unfortunately not extremely durable and many examples of this type do not survive.  China Galland in her book, *Love Cemetery, Unburying the Secret History of Slaves*, relates that graves were sometimes marked with things that were readily at hand.  For example a farmer may have a plow point placed on his grave, a seamstress a sewing machine part. [9]  Of course these items are long gone today but it may not be such a stretch to believe early graves here in Ontario were sometimes marked in the same way.

Stone markers were soon being used which, during the last decade of the eighteenth century, developed a particular rectangular style prominent during the entire nineteenth century. [10] These stones were so distinctive it is easy to distinguish them from their later  block-like counterparts introduced in the early 1900's. The early markers were made of marble or limestone with  marble  being  the  most  common.   In  the  nineteenth  century, Ontario produced a number of different limestones  which were  used in gravestones and of which  Kingston,  Ottawa  and  Queenston  varieties were most popular. [11]  Marble was generally imported from Vermont, a good source of blue marble .  C. Bounsall, a  monument carver in Bowmanville advertised for  both Italian and American marble monuments.    By the  1880's granite became the preferred stone as it still remains today.

In the late eighteenth/early nineteenth century, stones began to take on a typical form;  three feet high, two feet wide and either of the slab or headstone variety. Generally slab stones differ from headstones in that they are placed flush against the ground while headstones are upright tablets placed at the head of the grave. [12]    Headstones are often accompanied by footstones, smaller stones placed  at the foot of the grave which may display the initials or name of the deceased.   Few, if any, footstones are still present *in situ* but from the examples noted, none displayed any type of design motif.   It is difficult to say whether the lack of any motif on footstones was the norm because of the lack of existing examples.

Some form of design was usually applied to the upper portion of the stone, usually identified as the primary or  predominant  motif. Below  that would  appear  the biographical information of the deceased.   This information would often consist of the  person's age to the day, the name of the  parents and in the case of a married female,  her maiden name. An epitaph may appear in the lower portion of the stone. The sides of the stone may be embellished with floral or geometric shapes.

In many cases a small maker's mark was found in the lower left hand corner. These marks most often indicate the place where the stone was carved and the initials or full name of the carver may also be present (see left). Some stones in Connecticut even have prices listed.[13] How common was the practice of signing stones is difficult to ascertain since many of the stones have sunk into the ground making it impossible to determine the existence of these marks. However a study in Euphrasia Township, Grey County, Ontario shows 111 of 700 gravestones or 15.8% had makers' marks indicating place of origin.[14]

Gravestone carvings feature varying degrees of intricacy and craftsmanship. In the early days of settlement the person carving the stones could be a blacksmith, farmer or cooper who carved stones as needed. Carving stones would not have been profitable when there was not much demand and for many would have been only a supplementary occupation. All work was done using chisels and wooden mallets which required a very steady hand. Inscriptions and designs were drawn directly on the surface of the stone or a coating made of acacia-gum glue and plaster was used.[15]

The very earliest stones were rather crudely done when compared to later examples. The spacing of the letters was uneven and rarely is any motif or epitaph present. Instead biographical information is limited to the person's name, date of death and sometimes age at death. More than likely a friend or relative was commissioned to carve a suitable stone in the case of some of the very earliest stones. The David Coryell (1837) stone in the Pioneer Memorial Cemetery may be an example of such a stone. It is plain with no motifs present and crudely carved lettering. It was also common for stones dating from the 1820's and exhibiting some carving to have been manufactured at a later date and backdated.

Professional carvers were known to have set up business in several American cities by the early 1700s and the "Stone Cutter of Boston" was producing stones as early as 1653.[16] As for Oshawa it is difficult to determine when a stone cutter first established a business in the town. The County of Ontario Directory of 1869-1870 does not list any stone cutters or marble dealers in Oshawa. A survey of the Oshawa Vindicator newspapers for the years 1862-1871 also does not uncover any advertisements for stone cutters and evidence suggests there was not a professional stone cutter operating in Oshawa until much later in the nineteenth century

Many examples of gravestones in Oshawa display the craftsman's name and home town, however a mark indicating "Oshawa" was not seen until 1879 on the stone of Frankie Barker in Farewell Cemetery and 1880 on Teneck Boyns Robinson's stone located in the

Harbour Pioneer Cemetery.   Marks were seen indicating the  carving  was  done  in  places  as far  away  as  Whitby,  Bowmanville,  Newcastle and Toronto.    Darrell Norris in his study of  105 rural Ontario cemeteries suggests the median distance gravestones  were  shipped  was  twenty miles  with  at  least 10%  being  shipped  more  than  seventy-five  miles.[17] Considering the rudimentary transportation systems in place in  the  early  part  of  the  nineteenth  century transporting stones such a distance must have been quite an undertaking. However  a  lack  of  a professional carver in town  does not appear to be a hindrance to having a stone. It is not likely stones would have been ordered from such distances if there was   a professional carver in the immediate vicinity.

The  earliest  stone  discovered  in  Oshawa  with  a maker's mark was that of John and Nancy Henry, 1838 made by McD and M. of Newcastle.   By the mid 1850's the firm of J.J. Wolfenden Stone Cutters and Monument Dealers was in business in  Whitby. Several  stones  in the  cemeteries display a mark of J.J. and R.W., Whitby, the earliest being a child's stone from 1853.   These examples were probably the work  of  Johnathan and Richard Wolfenden.    Other Wolfendens  working with marble included Albert and William.   The Wolfenden's arrived in Canada in the mid to late 1850's and by the 1861 census Johnathon (1827-1885) had already established himself as a marble dealer.

WHITBY
STEAM MARBLE WORKS.
J. WOLFENDEN,
WHOLESALE AND RETAIL DEALER IN FOREIGN AND AMERICAN
MARBLE MANTELS, MONUMENTS, &c., &c.
DUNDAS STREET, WHITBY, ONT.
ALSO, AGENT FOR THE SCOTTISH GRANITE.

In  1857  Mr. Christopher  Bounsall (1817 – 1887) established  Bounsall's  Marble  and Granite   Works   in Bowmanville  shortly after arriving from England where he learned his trade. By 1886, Bounsall's Marble Works covered a ¼ of an acre on Division street in Bowmanville and employed six workers.   At least two of his children, Fred and Edwin, followed in his trade. Mr. Bounsall  advertised  in  the  Ontario  Reformer  newspaper ( June 28, 1872) and undoubtedly received much work from the area judging by the number of stones displaying "Bowmanville" in their lower left hand corner.

By 1880 Henry L. Godfray was operating a marbleworks in Oshawa. Godfray, born in Jersey, Channel Islands in 1838 operated the Dominion Stone and Marbleworks in Montreal as early as 1866 according to the McKays Montreal Directory.  The business was located on Bleury Street and later on Alexander Street.  Godfray was listed as a marblecutter in Toronto in the City Directory 1879 with his business at DeGrassi Street.

At the same time Godfray was operating in Oshawa there was another marble business in town, that of Anderson and Vanzant as seen on Maurice Morris stone (1879) in St. George's Cemetery. Alonzo Anderson (1848-1908) and Elias Vanzant (1852-1936) were brother in laws (Alonzo married Elias' sister Almira). Both men were from The Uxbridge area and started their business in Oshawa around 1880. Their business doesn't appear to have lasted for long here. In 1891 Anderson was a marble dealer in Toronto and Vanzant had moved to Grey County where he was also a marble dealer.

BOUNSALL'S MARBLE & GRANITE WORKS, BOWMANVILLE, ONT.

From the Northumberland and Durham County Historical Atlas 1878

In addition to the ability and preferences of the local carvers, another important factor to consider when searching for sources of inspiration for motif designs, is the preference by certain carvers for particular designs. Whether a stonecutter used personal whim or was guided by some theory in design is a matter of speculation. One stonecutter in the northeastern United States, when attempting to explain his design preferences, commented, "I continue to ornament my gravestones with vines, flowers and various little devices appropriate, as I thought, to the tomb; but, in truth there was much of it more whim than meaning."[18] Where would a carver turn for sources of inspiration? Several source books were available in the United States which show graphic images of coffins, Father Time, scythes, hourglasses, birds and the Tree of Life. There are numerous examples in the eastern seaboard area of the United States which appear to have been directly influenced by images in these books. It is feasible carvers in Ontario were also influenced by the same books whether directly or indirectly through American gravestone designs. One stone in Boston dating from 1678 used Francis Quarles' *Hieroglyphikes of the Life of Man* (1638) as inspiration. Trask mentions the possibility the winged angel heads may have as their source popular publications which were in circulation throughout North America.[19] Engraved illustrations in magazines and novels such as Joseph Addison's Spectator published in early 1700s, were probable sources of inspiration. Such publications were known for their portrayals of morality. It is possible carvers in Ontario would have had books or drawings of designs from which individuals would have chosen motifs similar to those in use today.

The square and compass is the most commonly seen
symbol of Freemasonry. Union Cemetery, Oshawa

# PREVIOUS RESEARCH

*"Some people felt that what I was beginning to study was merely quaint, much like hand embroidered valentines. I was told the old stones had no meaning and their study had best be left to amateur antiquarians."*

~ Allan I. Ludwig

Harriet Forbes produced the first major work in the field of gravestone research when she recorded and photographed the work of several early New England stone cutters. Published in 1927, *Gravestones of Early New England and the Men Who Made Them* was, an important volume on the study of carving traditions in New England however the subject of symbolism was not discussed in any detail. [20] Forbes looked at motifs from the point of their relationship to Christianity only and no other meanings linking culture or society were attempted.

It was not until the 1960s when gravestone iconography began to emerge as a legitimate field of historical research. Foremost in the literature was Allan Ludwig's seminal work, *Graven Images*, in which Ludwig introduced the idea of an iconographic tradition which exhibited stylistic change over time. For the first time iconography was viewed not as a static element but as an ever changing reflection of societal, and in particular, religious views. Basing his theory on Erwin R. Goodenough's work, *Jewish Symbols in the Greco-Roman Period*, Ludwig illustrated how the religious lives of the Puritans could be evaluated by examining the visual images they created. The Puritans created thousands of designs of angels and souls which Ludwig believed, represented a communication between man and God.[21] He uses the transformation of the death's head (skull) motif into a softer, cherub- like symbol as an indication of a shift in the religious values of the Puritans. During the seventeenth century, the skull effigy was the predominant motif present on New England gravestone. However by the eighteenth century this fearsome image was replaced by a winged soul represented by a cherub figure, which symbolized a life to come in the hereafter. Ludwig believed this iconographic change represented a shift in Puritan religious thought from emphasizing the life departed to the hope for the life to come. For several years the transitional images appear as neither skulls or souls, but a combination of both.[22]

This idea of change occurring as a continuum was further discussed by James Deetz and Edwin Dethlefsen, two anthropologists studying stylistic change in a Colonial Boston cemetery [31]. Deetz and Dethlefsen were testing the theory gravestones exhibit design variations in time and space which can be correlated with historical data. On stones dating from the 17th century they also noticed the predominance of the death's head as the main motif which over time underwent a simplification in design. The resulting cherub motifs occur mainly on stones dating after the mid 18th century and they too also underwent stylistic change leading to further simplification in design. By the end of the 18th century the appearance of the urn and willow appears almost exclusively as the chosen motif. Deetz and Dethlefsen recorded the shift away from the winged death head common on early stones to a predominance of cherubs images which in time gave way to willow and urn motifs. To explain these changes they looked to the religious views of the New Englanders and discovered a correlation between the decline in the strictness of the Orthodox Puritans and the stark portrayals of the winged death heads or skulls. As this decline intensified, gravestones began to exhibit softer, more ethereal designs such as cherubs. The further society moved away from strict religious expressions, the more secularized gravestone designs represented by images such as the willow or urn, appeared [32]. Deetz and Dethlefsen argued death's heads and cherubs are personalized representations unlike the urn and willow which are depersonalized.

The early death's head figure (top) gave way over time to the more ethereal cherub figure (below). Images from http://cdm.reed.edu/cdm4/indianconverts/studyguides/reading_gravestones/parts_gravestone.php

Researchers of gravestones in the northeastern region of the United States have made some great strides into the study of the symbolic meaning of the stones and changing stylistic trends. In Canada however, the idea of stylistic change over time has not been explored as extensively as in the New England region. Research in this country has typically focused on the style of Iconography and its various manifestations, or on the gravestone carving tradition. Although imagery on the nineteenth century Ontario gravestones was most certainly influenced to some extent by the New England traditions, several designs are not present in Ontario. For example the death's head and winged cherub are not native to Ontario stones. Large parts of Ontario were first settled by the end of the eighteenth century after the popularity of these particular styles had begun to diminish. Gravestone studies in Canada must account for the unique aspects of the tradition as it developed here while at the same time acknowledge the influences from New England.

One of the first major studies devoted to Ontario gravestones was Carole Hanks' *Early Ontario Gravestones*, which was the first attempt in Ontario to categorize motifs based on design. Largely a pictorial work , Hanks purpose was not to question the stylistic changes occurring with regards to the motifs but to focus on a detailed analysis of symbolic meanings for many motifs. The categorization system will be discussed further below. Several other studies on the east coast of Canada have produced illustrated inventories of several early cemeteries. Deborah Trask's work in Nova Scotia has little relevance for Ontario stones due to the strong New England influence with regards to motif styles.

At least two classification systems have been produced for Ontario gravestones but on their own merits neither can be described as a suitable model for use on a province wide basis. One example is the inventory sheet produced by Victor Konrad and Darrell Norris for their study of more than 5,000 Ontario gravestones in 105 rural cemeteries.[23] Studying stones from the period 1800-1909 Konrad and Norris wanted to establish a systematic and flexible approach to categorizing the stones based on elements such as form and motif style . In attempting to categorize the motifs Konrad and Norris developed a classification system of 8 motifs plus categories for "other" and "absent". Although initially intending to establish a "flexible" system for classifying these motifs, Konrad and Norris instead developed a rigid and narrowly focused system which I would argue does not allow for much variation of expression. Within the eight motif styles indicated are several which it can be argued, are variations of the same motif. For example, the categories of clasped and pointing hands (categories 3 and 4 respectively) represent different manifestations of the same style of motif . The same is true for the motifs of obelisk, urn and willow (categories 1,2 and 6 respectively) which belong to the same category because they represent similar symbolic meanings. Thistle (category 7) is the only floral element used and lamb (category 8) the only animal motif represented. By narrowly defining many of the motifs, Konrad and Norris have had to put a significant number of motifs in the "other" category which encompasses such styles as trees, angels and obelisks. In the period 1860-1869 13.4% of the motifs were delegated to the other category and in 1900-1909 a substantial 20.2% of motifs were so classified.    In  at  least  six  of  their  nine  reporting  periods  a  minimum 10% of stones were classified as "other".[24]


Testing this categorization system in Oshawa, Ontario revealed  many  of  the  motifs  did not  fit  into  the  categories resulting in a disproportionate amount of entries for   "other". For example, one of the  most  popular  styles  of  motif  is represented by floral expressions which are not necessarily thistles, a floral variety usually reserved for those of Scottish descent.   Where would these motifs be placed other than in the "other" category?   Categorizing motifs from the level of their symbolic meanings rather than  merely  their  artistic  expression  allows  for  a more  precise  and  accurate classification. The  results  of  their  study  indicate  a  definite preference for willow and urn motifs prior to  1840 although all the main motifs were seen in varying amounts.   The most popular motifs continued to be the willow and urn throughout the 1840's and  1850's and the hand of God for the period 1840  through 1900.    Konrad  and Norris  also  notice  an increasing popularity for motifs representing a secular image of death being used by the end of the century.   These motifs would be represented by floral motifs rather than  symbols specifically relating to mourning or religion.


By  far  the  best  categorization  system  proposed  for Ontario appears in *Early Ontario Gravestones* by Carol Hanks published in  1974.   Although the purpose of her study was  not  to develop  a  gravestone  classification  system,  Hanks  was  the  first  to  recognize  the importance  of  a standardized classification approach to gravestones based on iconography. She identified six categories of motifs; classical revival,  hands,  flowers,  animals  and  angels  with the  sixth  category,  miscellaneous,  to  account  for  all  other  motifs.    It is simple and bases categorization on symbolic meanings of the carvings. Although  many  of  her  observations  and conclusions  are  influenced  by  her  background  in  art,  with some  minor  revisions  in terminology, this system  could  be used  as  a  basis  to  develop  a  province wide classification system.   For example, instead of "angels" I would suggest the category name be revised to "figures" to represent both human and  divine  figures Flowers would be changed to "floral" to accommodate  all  the  expressions  represented  by wreaths, garlands and thistles which are not always flowers. Finally,  a  seventh  category  "motif-less"  or  "absent"  should  be  added  to accommodate  the  stones  on  which  a  motif  is intentionally absent as opposed to missing due to disrepair or    disintegration. The    seven    categories, floral, classical revival, hands, animal, figure, motif-less and miscellaneous,   would , I believe, accommodate  the  majority  of gravestone  iconography appearing on nineteenth century Ontario gravestones.

# Method

*The fence around a cemetery is foolish, for those inside can't get out
and those outside don't want to get in.*

~Arthur Brisbane

Several cemeteries were chosen for testing the viability of the classification system. All the cemeteries are located within Oshawa, Ontario, a city of approximately 152,000 people situated 60 kilometers east of Toronto. The cemeteries, Pioneer Memorial, Harbour Pioneer, Farewell, Union and St. George's Anglican, were chosen because they represent five of the oldest cemeteries in the area and contain the burials of some of the earliest settlers. These cemeteries also contain the largest collection of slab/headstones still surviving in Oshawa.

The primary data for the study was the motifs appearing on the markers in the cemeteries. The majority of the gravestones used were of the slab or headstone variety, however other styles, where present, were included. As this classification system is for nineteenth century gravestones, only those stones from the period 1800-1899 were used because, as mentioned previously, stones underwent some major changes in form and style after this date. To determine the extent of stylistic change over time only those stones which could be dated to a specific decade were utilized.

As illustrated in Table 1, more than 300 stones were analyzed in total to illustrate the most popular motifs in a decade and the existence, if any, of patterns. The stones were carefully recorded listing all pertinent information including name, death date, sex, age at death and style of motif present. Sex and age at death were used in some cases to determine if there was a correlation between a popular motif and the deceased's age and/or sex. This was especially useful when examining children's stones. If more than one death date was indicated on the stone the last death date was used for dating purposes. Stones were not used if a death date was not present or if the motif could not be identified with certainty. To augment the gravestones personally recorded, transcription records with details of motifs from the Oshawa Community Museum for St. George's, Farewell and Pioneer Memorial Cemeteries were used. In addition many cemetery studies from Ontario were utilized to ascertain the validity of the proposed classification system on a province wide basis.

Table 1 Number of Stones Studied

| CEMETERY | Number of Stones |
|---|---|
| Farewell | 22 |
| Union | 83 |
| Pioneer | 136 |
| Harbour | 24 |
| St George's | 53 |
| Total | 318 |

In cases where more than one motif was present, predominant and secondary motifs were classified. The predominant motif was used for comparison and was defined as the motif located in the centre of the stone and/or the largest motif. Any of the categories could be predominant motifs when appearing alone. However, some categories, when used in combination with others, were consistently classified as secondary. This would occur particularly with floral motifs. When floral motifs appeared in combination with another motif style, floral was always viewed as a secondary motif which merely acted as a decorative detail for the other motif.

# Motif Categories

*Redeem the misspent time that's past*
*Live each day as it were thy last*
*And of thy talents take great care*
*For the last day thyself prepare*
*Live mindful of death. 1801*

~Jean Dick sampler
Collection of the Oshawa Community Museum

As discussed earlier, the classification system proposed is based in part on Carole Hanks' work *Early Ontario Gravestones* which outlined a tentative system for classifying gravestones in Ontario. The classification system proposed herein modifies Hanks' conclusions to allow for a simpler and, I believe, more flexible approach to studying gravestone motifs on nineteenth century Ontario stones. Although there is an immense array of expressions exhibited on gravestones, I believe only seven categories are required to accommodate the vast majority of motifs. The categories proposed are as follows; hands, floral, classical revival, figures, animals, miscellaneous and motif-less (none) Each category, along with its common manifestations, will be discussed in more detail and illustrated with examples from Oshawa cemeteries.

*Pioneer Memorial Cemetery, Oshawa*

# Hands

*In Reason's ear they all rejoice, And utter forth a glorious voice, For ever singing, as they shine: 'The hand that made us is divine.*

~ Joseph Addison
In The Spectator, no.465, 23 Aug

Motifs featuring hands appear frequently in all the cemeteries chosen for study and are ubiquitous throughout early Ontario cemeteries. Table 2 illustrates the frequency of the hand motifs in the Oshawa cemeteries.

Symbolically hands represent an expression of a relationship, most commonly between the living and the dead.[25] The hand motif can be further subdivided into four sub categories each with its own meaning; hand pointing upwards, hand descending from the sky, clasping hands and upwards presenting hands.[26] The most common manifestation seen in the Oshawa examples, as indicated in Table 3, is with the first finger of the right hand pointing upwards indicating the pathway traveled of the deceased to heaven. Sometimes the hand is facing away from the viewer but most often the hand appears with the palm and fingers exposed. Although popular throughout the nineteenth century the upwards pointing hand appears to be most predominate in the decades 1860, 1870 and 1880, an observation supported by Nancy Patterson in her study. This motif is often accompanied by a short epitaph such as "There is Rest in Heaven" (stone of Elizabeth Dundas, 1862) or Gone But not Forgotten" (stone of Janet Ketchen, 1861) and may be set inside a rondel (a decorative plate in round form). When attempting to define the meaning of the upward pointing hand, the epitaphs which accompany some of the examples may provide some clues.

*Elizabeth Dundas stone is an example of the upwards pointing hand*

In all cases observed in Oshawa, the epitaphs refer either to a parting such as "Gone Home" or to heaven. It is likely the hand is indicating the way the deceased's soul has traveled in death (heavenwards). The hope for the deceased to travel to heaven probably accounts for the popularity of the hand on modern markers as well.

Hands which are linked or clasping one another as in a handshake are another common manifestation of this motif type. Patterson found linked hands were the most numerous and longest lasting of the hand motifs. [27] From the right side of the tablet extends the right hand which is generally the one clasping the hand extending from the left The handshake may appear to be quite firm where both hands are grasping equally strongly ( the stone of Carrie Wright, 1877, is an excellent example of a firm handshake) or can appear as if the right hand is clasping the left hand to lead them somewhere ( stone of James Fewster, 1883). It is difficult to ascertain if the various expressions of linked hands denote meaning or were merely representing the skill or whim of the carver. Several meanings have been suggested by which the clasping hands signify union or represent a symbol of greeting with the hope of meeting loved ones again.

Table 2   Frequency of Hand Motifs by Cemetery

| CEMETERY | Number of Stones (% of total in cemetery) |
|----------|-------------------------------------------|
| Farewell | 3 (13.6) |
| Union | 31 (37.3) |
| Pioneer | 13 (9.5) |
| Harbour | 4 (17.3) |
| St George's | 1(1.8) |
| Total | 52 |

The stones of husband and wife Alexander and Harriet Greig in Union cemetery at first glance, seem to suggest such a hereafter reunion (see page 8). Situated side by side the stones are nearly identical in detail suggesting they were carved by the same person and exhibit the same clasping hand motif. On closer inspection the hands on Alexander Greig's stone are clasped in a firm handshake suggesting a willingness on the part of both parties to meet. On Harriet Greig's stone the hand extending from the right is clasping the left hand as if to lead the way. Had the death dates been reversed this might have been a case for a husband or wife greeting their life partner in the hereafter. Common to all these suggestions is the idea of union whereby loved ones are united in spirit even though they must be separated physically. In cases where the stone belongs to a member of a fraternal order such as the Masons, linked hands may indicate an expression of fraternity or allegiance. [28]

Although not as popular as the upward pointing and linked hands motifs, the upwards presenting hands does appear consistently enough in the nineteenth century to warrant its own sub category. Patterson's sample shows a predominance for the presenting hands beginning in the 1880's and continuing through to the 1900s. [29] In the Oshawa study presenting hands peak somewhat earlier in the 1860s and 1870s. Presenting hands are usually holding a Bible as in the cases of Norris Kerr's (1860) and Arthur Kirkpatrick's (1874) stones or flowers as seen on the stones of Emma Morgan (below) or Elizabeth Pascoe.

A hand descending as if from the sky is the rarest of the four sub-categories of hand motifs. This expression of the presenting hand is treated separately from the upwards presenting hand because of what I believe is the different symbolic connotation of the hand. Whereas the upward presenting hand more than likely represents the hand of the deceased offering a token or words of wisdom to the living, the descending hand represents symbolically the hand of God. The hand is generally holding an object, usually a scroll with a message for the living. There are two such stones in Oshawa, both appear strikingly similar, leading one to believe they were carved by the same person. Both Rachel Kerr's (1865, see below) and George Lovell's (1862, see next page) stones exhibit a hand descending from the top of the stone through drapes and holding a scroll. Lovell's scroll reads "We part in hope to meet again" and Kerr's simply states "To memory dear". Upside down torches flank the sides of the stones in both cases. The similarities in the motifs may indicate they were carved by the same craftsman

Table 3  Frequency of Hand Motifs by Type

| Type of Hand Motif | % of Hand Motifs in Cemeteries |
|---|---|
| Pointing Up | 55.7% |
| Pointing Down | 3.8% |
| Clasping | 32.6% |
| Presenting | 7.6% |
| Total | 99.7%* |

*May not equal 100 due to rounding.

# Classical Revival

*Adieu, adieu, kind friends, adieu, adieu, adieu, / I can no longer stay with you, stay with you. / I'll hang my harp on a weeping willow-tree. / And may the world go well with thee."*

~ The Tavern Song

The classical revival motifs, manifesting as columns, urns, willow trees and obelisks, began to appear on Oshawa area gravestones by the 1830s. This is similar in time to their appearance in Nova Scotia where willows and urns were seen by 1830. This is somewhat later, however, than areas of the eastern seaboard of the United States where neoclassical symbols were firmly entrenched by the time of the War of 1812. The willow tree was the most commonly used classical revival symbol in Oshawa. In Christian legend the willow tree is a symbol of longevity, flourishing despite being cut. It is the symbol of the gospel of Christ which remained intact despite being widely distributed. The willow tree however also carries a romantic, sentimental connotation by appearing to "weep" which represents the sorrow and grief associated with death. In several examples the willow tree is depicted slightly off centre as if leaning or weeping over an urn or coffin.

The willow tree can be depicted alone or in combination with other motifs most notably urns, obelisks or coffins. Urns and obelisks especially are classically inspired images. As funerary objects, urns were utilized during the 1800's but were borrowed from Greek mythology where they were utilized as a receptacle for human remains.[30]

Although classical revival motifs may appear in the cemeteries as "monotonous and nearly identical"[31], several interesting manifestations are represented in Oshawa cemeteries. As indicated previously the most prevalent classical revival motif appearing in Oshawa is the willow tree depicted either by itself or, more commonly, with another motif such as an urn. Several stones show a willow tree/figure combination which will be discussed in the section under "figures". The willow tree/urn combination is a "classic" manifestation of revival motifs. The stone of William and Marg Garfat 1865/1866 as shown on page 29 displays an urn flanked by two willow trees possibly representing the two deceased. Emily Luke's stone (1841) shows a large willow with an urn to the right. The motif is well carved illustrating clearly the 'weeping' nature of the tree and the clear, crisp lines for the urn. The Luke stone is one of the few examples where the willow tree is shown larger than the urn. In the majority of willow tree/urn combinations the urn is vastly out of proportion appearing much larger than the tree (see Robert Taylor stone page 30).    This is also the case for willow tree/obelisk combinations.   With the stones of Eliza Wood (1855), Elizabeth Vansickler (1854) , Richard Venstone (1854) and Martha Clark(1860) the obelisks are flanked by willow trees which are the same height or obviously smaller than the obelisks.   Whether this was a deliberate attempt at symbolism on the part of the carver and/or those who commissioned the stone is mere conjecture.   Perhaps this was a deliberate attempt to portray the obelisk as the predominate motif.

Table 4   Frequency of Classical Revival Motifs

| CEMETERY | Number of Stones (% of total in cemetery) |
|---|---|
| Farewell | 7 (31.8) |
| Union | 26 (31.3) |
| Pioneer | 29 (21.3) |
| Harbour | 2 (8.6) |
| St George's | 1 (1.8) |
| Total | 65 |

The classical revival inspired motif is an excellent example of a popular trend in visual arts  influencing gravestone symbolism.  The popularity of these designs can be linked to a fervent interest in anything Greek or Roman which   was   sweeping   North America   during   the   late eighteenth and   early nineteenth century.   The Neoclassical period 1760-1780 is associated  with  Robert  Adams, architect, interior designer and furniture designer, who was  inspired by classical antiquity.   He utilized patera, Greek key, anthemion, fan, urn and cameo motifs in his designs  . Gradually  the  Neoclassical  was replaced   by   the   Rococo influence during  the  last  years  of  the  eighteenth  and  early nineteenth centuries.    This period, commonly referred to as Federal in the United States (1795-1820), saw gravestones become less of a religious artistic expression and more of a showcase of what was happening in popular culture.

As   mentioned   previously   Greek   and   Roman archaeological finds were a strong influence on popular culture at the time influencing designs in architecture, clothing,  interior  design  and  of  course  gravestones. Excavations at Pompeii were conducted during the early 19<sup>th</sup> century and were covered extensively in the media. Examples of wall paintings depict decorative elements such as columns, grape vines and cupids with bows and arrows all later seen incorporated as gravestone motifs.   Many of the paintings also depict figures floating or hovering in the sky. Dressed in flowing robes and carrying wands or musical instruments, these figures are reminiscent of the divine figures portrayed on gravestones.   One of the most striking examples is of a *maenad*, a follower of the god Dionysus, who is shown on a wall painting as floating through the sky with a long flowing robe giving the impression of wings.[32]   Looking at the depictions from the archaeological finds one can certainly see the influence for gravestone design.

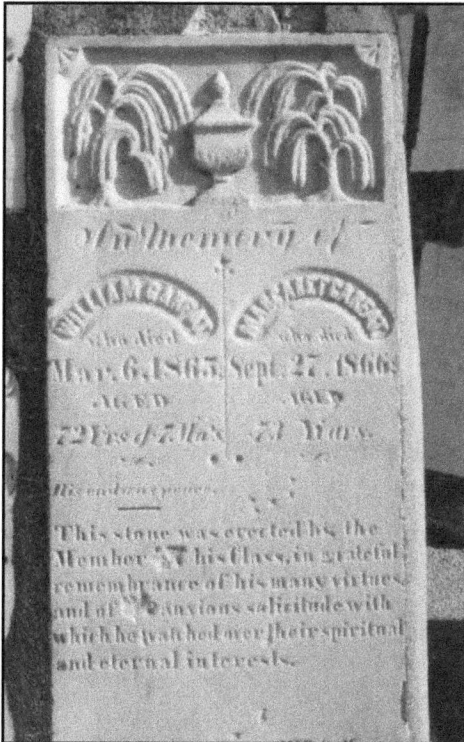

Evidence of classical revival designs are most visible during the period 1800-1830 in Ontario but continue to dominate much longer in the more rural areas.   In Oshawa the first example of a classical revival inspired motif does not appear until the 1830s, peaks in the 1850s and 1860s  with few appearing after 1869 and none appearing after the 1880s.[33] This is somewhat later than the period  of popularity in other areas such as the United States where the willow  tree was introduced as early as the first half of the eighteenth century and peaked in popularity during the early part of the nineteenth century.   In Nova Scotia the classic revival period of gravestone design begins in the 1830s and extends  through the 1840s and into the 1850s. As interest in the Greek/Roman period waned towards the latter part of the nineteenth century so too did the  presence  of classical designs, in particular willow trees.

      In Oshawa, classical revival motifs are behind only floral and sometimes hand motifs in popularity.  In fact in the Farewell and Union cemeteries, classical revival motifs account for over 31% of the motifs present and in the Pioneer Memorial over 21%. The only exception to this popularity trend is reflected in St. George's Anglican cemetery where they occur on less than  2% of the stones. Reasons for this apparent lack of affinity for classical revival motifs will be discussed further under the section for St. George's Anglican cemetery.

*Robert (left) and Margaret (right) Taylor's stones are excellent examples of classical revival motifs. Both feature weeping willow trees and Robert's has a large urn.*

# Figures

*I saw the angel in the marble and carved until I set him free.*

~Michelangelo

Motifs representing figures, both human and divine, are rare in Oshawa (Table 5) and Ontario in general. When classifying this particular motif as rare it should be stressed that these motifs do appear in Ontario cemeteries but not to the extent they are seen on the eastern seaboard of the United States or in Nova Scotia. Often when they do appear it is in conjunction with other motif styles, particularly classical revival. Human figures are defined by Stone and Russell as those figures representing persons, excluding portrait stones, and may include representations of allegorical figures such as Adam and Eve.[34] Of the human figures the mourning female, often carved as kneeling, leaning or crouching, is most common. Male figures are extremely uncommon. Divine figures represent winged soul/cherub effigies and angels which may carry wreaths, scrolls and trumpets.

Table 5  Frequency of Figure Motifs by Cemetery

| CEMETERY | Number of Stones (% of total in cemetery) |
|----------|-------------------------------------------|
| Farewell | 1 (4.5) |
| Union | 0 |
| Pioneer | 2 (1.5) |
| Harbour | 0 |
| St George's | 1 (1.8) |
| Total | 4 |

Figure motifs represent less than 2% of all gravestone motifs in the cemeteries studied. In fact no figures were seen on tombstones in Union Cemetery and in Pioneer Cemetery only 2 of the 136 (1.5%) stones and 1 of 53 stones in St. George's (1.8%) actually contained figures, whether human or divine, representing the sole or main motif image. However several stones did have figures used in conjunction with other motifs particularly classical revival. For the purpose of discussion these stones will be included, however they are not included in any statistical analysis   These numbers appear to be fairly typical of Ontario cemeteries as Stone and Russell estimate only 10% of all early Ontario cemeteries   actually  have  any figures  represented  on tombstones.[35]  In contrast Deborah Trask reports angels and cherubs appear as the most popular image in the  early 1800s in Nova Scotia.[36]

In the Oshawa cemeteries the most common figures portrayed were divine beings, notably angels, as opposed to humans.    All of the figures reported were of angels with   two notable  exceptions. The  sole  human  mourning  figure represented  was  discovered  on the stone of Julia Wright (1858).   The small stone depicts a  clearly female figure  in long  skirts weeping  into  a  handkerchief  over  a  small headstone  or  possibly  obelisk (see below). Likely  the  figure represents   a   maternal   presence   as   the   genealogical information indicates the deceased was a two year old girl. The second exception is the Richard Venstone stone  (1853) where an angel is portrayed as a cherub figure, a common depiction in the northeast United States but not particularly for Ontario.   Also unusual is the fact the angel  is depicted standing on the ground and not "hovering" as in all the other examples.

Angels are featured in combination with classical revival motifs on several stones including Elizabeth Vansickler (willow tree and obelisk), Eliza Brigham (willow tree) and Eliza Ann Wood (willow tree and obelisk). Mary (Dearborne) Lamb's stone (1855) is a rare example of an angel appearing as the predominate motif . An angel in flowing dress and large wings carries a scroll simply stating "Arise" as she hovers over a coffin. In this example the angel is undoubtedly acting as the guardian which transports the soul to heaven. Elizabeth Susan (Hyland) McBrien's stone (1871) also features an angel as the predominant motif. The beautiful angel figure was depicted with wings and a long flowing robe, cradling a baby and pointing upwards. Research indicates Elizabeth died on February 2, 1871, a week after giving birth to her daughter Minnie McBrien on January 26, 1871. Elizabeth's husband, Alfred Nelson McBrien was a doctor and in the 1871 census is listed as widowed with a three month old daughter. The angel glancing over her shoulder may convey a message to the mortals assuring them the pathway travelled for the deceased is heavenwards (see below).

*St. George's Anglican Cemetery, Oshawa.*

*Photo by Melissa Cole*

# Floral

*Flowers have spoken to me more than I can tell in written words. They are the hieroglyphics of angels, loved by all men for the beauty of the character, though few can decipher even fragments of their meaning.*

~Lydia M. Child

Floral motifs were by far, the most popular motifs seen in the graveyards of Oshawa.  In the nineteenth century, floral motifs were used both symbolically, to portray a certain meaning or sentiment and decoratively to enhance the stones. Often appearing in combination with other motifs, floral designs are sometimes added as a beautifying or decorative element to many stones.  It is for this reason floral elements are classified as secondary motifs unless they appear alone on the gravestone. However, as primary motifs, floral is behind only classical revival in popularity.  Unlike other motif styles such as fraternal affiliations and figures, examples of floral motifs appear in all the cemeteries studied.  The earliest examples were seen in the 1830's and continued to appear throughout the century into the 1880s. The flower may have been viewed as a `feminine' image and therefore used predominately on the stones of women and children. In the Harbour Pioneer cemetery,  23 of 24 primary floral motifs are on the stones of women and children. Similarly, in the Farewell cemetery, all nine floral examples were again for women and children.   If floral images were used on the stones of men it was often as a floral wreath instead of a single flower as shown on the stone of Thomas Guy (see next page).

Table 6   Frequency of Floral Motifs by Cemetery

| CEMETERY | Number of Stones (% of total in cemetery) |
|---|---|
| Farewell | 9 (40.9) |
| Union | 13 (15.6) |
| Pioneer | 24 (17.6) |
| Harbour | 5 (21.7) |
| St George's | 12 (22.6) |
| Total | 63 |

As a symbol, the flower has long been associated with commemoration of the dead and celebration of life. People send flowers to funerals as a tribute to the departed. In Job 14 man is compared to a flower, "man that is born of woman is of few days and full of trouble. He come forth like a flower and is cut down: he fleeth also a shadow and continuet not". [37] For the Victorians, each type of flower had a particular meaning and careful thought was put into making just the right choice. Today much of the meaning associated with various types of flowers is gone but for the Victorians flowers represented one more way to communicate. In Christian iconography, the lily and the rose represent purity and examples of foliage and fruit are suggestive of the lushness of heaven. The grapevine, a popular choice, represents Christ in the vine and followers in the branches. Ivy leaves refer to Christian constancy, laurel leaves to victory over evil and palm leaves to peace, victory and excellence. The daisy symbolized purity and peace and rosemary remembrance. The thistle is the national flower of Scotland and appears on the stones of many immigrants. Flowers also represent the beauty and brevity of life. A flower bud or broken bud was often used to indicate a life, usually a child's, which budded on earth but would bloom in heaven. Epitaphs such as this example proclaiming "This lovely bud so young and fair/called forth by early doom/Just came to show how sweet a flower/ In paradise would bloom" further expressed the notion of a life cut short." [38] Unfortunately due to poor gravestone condition, it is difficult in some cases to determine the type of flower depicted.

Floral motifs appeared in many variations including single flowers, wreaths, vines or particular types such as thistle. Often a floral wreath symbolizing mourning would frame a short epitaph such as "Gone Home" in the case of Richard and Mary Luke, (1869), or "There is Rest in Heaven" from the stone of James Tuttle, (1861). Due to their natural shape, wreaths were most often used in a sense of enclosing an epitaph. As a decorative element, flowers may be used in combination with any type of motif. Melinda Morrissy's stone (1877) is a particularly nice example of flowers used to complement the primary motif. In this case the principle motif is the clasping hands encircled with a wreath of flowers.

As the primary motif flowers may appear as a single flower as in the case of John and Ann Cooper's stone (1863) which features a single rose tied with a ribbon stating "In Memory" (below left).    The motif may be more elaborate as seen in Jessie Thornton's stone  (1869) where a bouquet of flowers tied with a ribbon is used (below right).

*Both stones are excellent examples of floral motifs*
*presenting as the primary motif.  Often floral motifs*
*will be used as accent or decorative motifs.*

# Animals

"And I said, Oh that I had wings like a dove for then would I fly away, and be at
rest."
~Bible Quotes

Religious symbolism involving animals goes back to the earliest days of religion.
Gravestone depictions of animals are mostly commonly seen on children's stones.
Although animal depictions are uncommon in adult gravestones, there was one seen in
the cemeteries studied.

Table 7   Frequency of Animal Motifs by Cemetery

| CEMETERY | Number of Stones (% of total in cemetery) |
|---|---|
| Farewell | 2 (9) |
| Union | 6 (7.2) |
| Pioneer | 8 (5.8) |
| Harbour | 3 (13.0) |
| St George's | 7 (13.2) |
| Total | 26 |

Most animal motifs are limited to birds, in particular doves, and lambs both
well known Christian symbols for devotion, purity and peace and in religion is a
symbol of the Holy Ghost.   The dove and the lamb were both viewed as particularly
well suited for the stones of children. Hanks speculates this frequency of animal
depictions on children's stones may indicate a less traditional meaning had evolved for
these two motifs one which rather than stressing a Christian meaning     stressed
youth   and   innocence . [39]     This   explanation   would   certainly   account   for   the
disproportionate number of appearances of animals on the children's stones since
children would be considered more innocent than adults.

Doves along with pigeons are part of the bird family *Columbidae* and often the terms
dove and pigeon are used interchangeably.  In religion, the dove represents the Holy

Ghost or the departed spirit and sometimes as a bearer of heavenly news. On gravestones, doves can appear alone or in combination with another motif, particularly of the floral type. The Isabella and Ida Hern stone (1860/1865) depicts a tragic display of a dove sitting on a branch gazing down on an obviously dead dove laying on the ground (below left). In another example two well illustrated doves carry a floral wreath heavenward (below right).

*One dove gazes down on the lifeless body of another.*

*Stone of Henrietta and William Clarkson features 2 doves shown carrying a wreath heavenwards. The dove is commonly seen on stones of children.*

In Christian art the lamb is often interpreted as the symbol for Christ representing innocence and purity. A lamb is the most frequently seen motif on children's stones. In several instances the lamb is portrayed as sleeping with the nose tucked under the front legs. There are also many cases, several of which appear in St George's Cemetery, where a lamb appears as a sculpture resting on top of the stone. Unfortunately the exposure of the sculpture renders it vulnerable to weathering leaving most of the detail eroded. On the stone of Hester Woods there still remains some suggestion of a graceful lamb with long ears and peaceful expression. Another popular manifestation of the lamb is in a sitting position accompanied by a floral wreath.

An unusual manifestation of the lamb is in combination with a tree, notably a willow. Hanks notes "rarely are animals found in combination with any tree motif and this (reference to the Edward Dukesbury stone in Brockville) is the only instance discovered of an animal depicted with a willow tree". [40] However there are at least two examples of an animal/willow tree pairing in Oshawa suggesting the combination may not be all that rare. The unusual nature of one of the examples found in Oshawa stems from the fact the lamb appears on the stone of a 56 year old male and not a child (see below). [41]

*John Stephenson stone in Pioneer Memorial Cemetery, depicts a lamb/willow tree combination. The lamb is most commonly associated with the stones of children.*

# Miscellaneous

*Visit the sick, relieve the distressed, bury the dead and educate the orphan."*

~Command of the Independent Order of Oddfellows

Although it is the intention of the classification system to categorize gravestones based on their motifs, there will be always be examples which, due to their unusual motifs or complex combinations, are more difficult to place in a category. Therefore a "catch-all" category known as miscellaneous, was created to cover motifs, which due to their individual expressions, do not easily fit into one of the other categories. These motifs often include designs relating to occupational status or affiliations with secret societies and organizations. Three of the five cemeteries contained stones which were best described under the miscellaneous category as illustrated in Table 8 .

Table 8   Frequency of Miscellaneous Motifs by Cemetery

| CEMETERY | Number of Stones (% of total in cemetery) |
|---|---|
| Farewell | 0 |
| Union | 7 (8.4) |
| Pioneer | 2 (1.4) |
| Harbour | 0 |
| St George's | 4 (7.5) |
| Total | 13 |

Fraternal Organizations

It has been estimated that in the 1920s more than 30 million people or over half the population of the United States belonged to at least one fraternal or secret benefit society.[42] The symbols and emblems of these organizations were seen on a variety of objects including furniture, jewelry and of course on gravestones. With over 2,000 fraternal societies believed to have been in existence in North America at least some of the time since the mid 1800s ascertaining the meaning or affiliation of a symbol may be difficult.

However several of the organizations do appear with some regularity on stones in Ontario particularly examples of motifs relating to membership in the Grand Lodge of Ancient Free and Accepted Masons of Canada. Freemasonry is the oldest and the largest fraternity in the world. Masons believe that each man has a responsibility to improve himself and remain devoted to family, faith, country and fraternity.

The Masons have a long history in Oshawa and vicinity. The first mention of a lodge is recorded for Whitby as early as 1808 .[43] Oshawa's Lebanon Lodge received its warrant in 1860 but membership records indicate many gentlemen from Oshawa were attending Unity Lodge in Whitby established since 1826 . As the oldest and most historically influential fraternal society, motifs relating to membership in the Masons were the most frequently observed affiliation represented on the gravestones. Examples of motifs may include an eye for watchfulness, sprig of acacia for immortality, an ark indicating passage through troubled times, an anchor for hope and the letter "G" for God and geometry representing spiritual and material worlds. However the most frequently observed symbol is the square and compass representing virtue and wisdom as seen on the stone of James Bain (1869, right) . Both the square and compass are tools of architect's trade used to create true lines and perfect angles. The stone masons also use the square and compass in their trade. When the square and compass is placed together with God (G), peace and harmony is the result.

The five examples from the Union Cemetery in Oshawa, all exhibited the square and compass motif. It is interesting to note not all members of the Masons were identified on their gravestones. In fact by cross referencing membership lists and cemetery records it is seen only a very small percentage of members had any identifiable Masonic symbols on their stones. Even the first Grand Master of Lebanon Lodge, Oshawa, Silas Fairbanks, is buried in Union Cemetery with no Masonic symbols on his gravestone. Often regarded as a secret society masons were not known to broadcast their association and it was not until fairly recently in the 20th century Masonic symbols were used with any frequency on stones. [44]

Another fraternal society observed in the cemeteries was the Independent Order of Oddfellows (IOOF), also known as the Three Link Fraternity. Oddfellows is composed of men, women and children who believe in a supreme being and that Friendship, Love and Truth are principles to live by. a group based loosely on the principles of freemasonry which incorporates its own membership ranks and symbolism. As IOOF and Free Masons were closely related, it is not uncommon to see symbols from both organizations on the same gravestone. In 1847 a lodge was instituted in Oshawa, the third in the province after Ottawa and Toronto. Although the first lodge, Rebekah, was not established until 1881, there were many members of IOOF in Oshawa prior. Newspapers reported in 1872 of the funeral of an Oddfellow and organ builder, William Robinson, who died at the age of 27 leaving behind a wife and a young child.[45] Fraternal organizations often acted in an early welfare capacity for their members which is illustrated by the circumstances of William Robinson. Although he was a relative newcomer in town, Robinson was cared for throughout his illness by

Oddfellows; "in the Robinson circumstance is illustrated some of the principle virtues of Oddfellowship. Mr Robinson was a stranger in our midst and being a member of the Brotherhood he was tenderly cared for when sick and honourably buried when life had flown." [46] and his funeral was attended by Brethren from Bowmanville, Oshawa and Whitby. The most frequently observed symbol on IOOF stones is the three links of chain representing Friendship, Love and Truth. Other symbols may include a shepherd's crook, clasped hands and a bow and arrow.

Order of the Eastern Star is today the largest fraternal organization in the world to which both men and women belong. In order to join the Order men must be Master Masons. The Order is not a religion but is comprised of people with spiritual beliefs brought together to help one another though the stated purposes of charitable, educational, fraternal and scientific. The most common motif is the five pointed Star with a tip pointing downwards representing the Star of Bethlehem but other less known, symbols may include a broken pillar, sheaf of wheat, chalice, draped sword and crown and scepter.

In some cases a motif may indicate an occupation. In the case of Reverend James Lambie an open Bible is a fitting tribute to a man of the cloth. Robert Rundle's stone from 1853 features an anchor inside a wreath. The anchor usually is symbolic of hope but in this case the epitaph may shed more light on the meaning. Stating "Safe landed on that shore, Where sailors must in ---------- over" the epitaph would suggest Mr. Rundle was a sailor or at least someone who loved the sea.

Some gravestones, which due to their complex combinations, are difficult to decipher and thus categorize. Such motifs are also placed in the miscellaneous category. One of the most difficult stones to decipher symbolically is the Robert Ormiston stone (1879, see next page) in Union Cemetery which features a dove flying upwards into two hands descending from behind drapes. In this particular example the dove and the hand appear to be equally important motifs and miscellaneous appeared to be most fitting. The dove most likely represents the soul of the deceased ascending to heaven into the welcoming hands of God. Symbolically the stone is certainly religious in its message. Another example of a stone placed in this category would be that of Ellen Rundle (1881). The heavy draped curtain possibly indicates the final act in life as the curtain of life appears to "come down". The curtain was seen on several stones and fits most appropriately in the miscellaneous category.

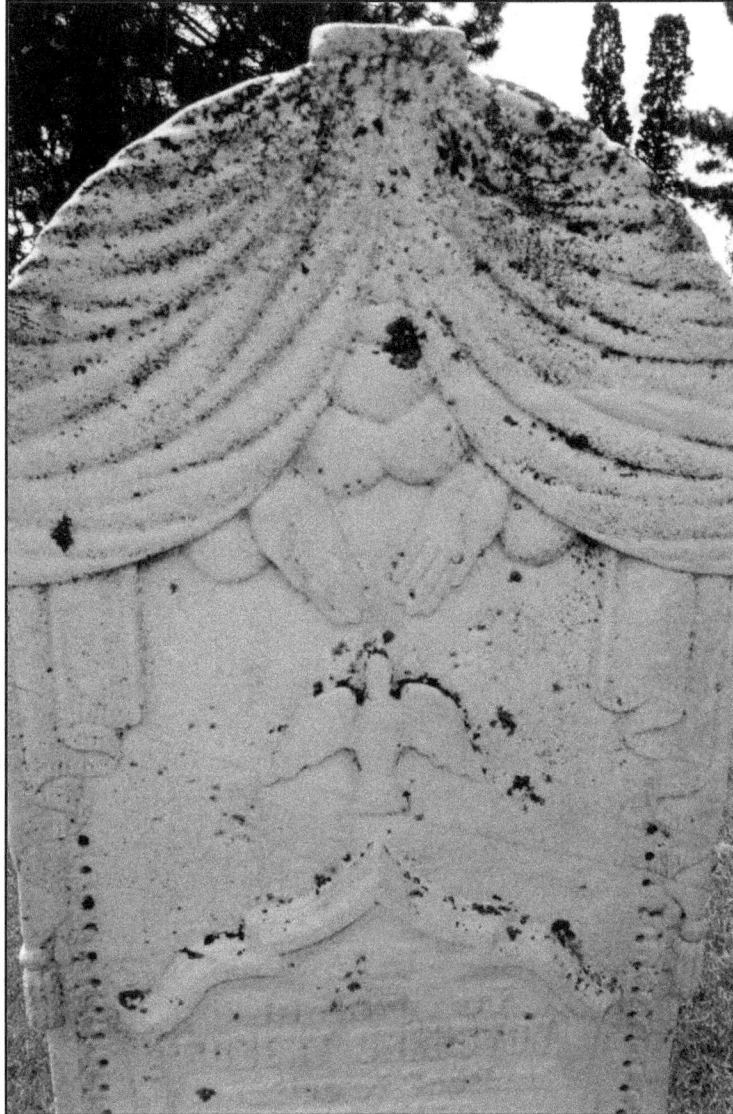

*Robert Ormiston's stone features several motifs including, the dove, descending hands and a curtain. The motifs are rich in meaning. For example the dove may represent the departed's soul being welcomed into Heaven. The curtain represents the final act.*

# Motif-less

*The close of the nineteenth century saw fewer Ontario gravestones decorated with motifs.*

*~Darrell Norris*

The final category, motif-less, is one I propose to cover the stones which intentionally exhibit no motif or design particularly in the latter half of the nineteenth century when access to carvers was generally more available. Gravestones with no motif may present the pertinent biographical information combined in some cases with a short epitaph as seen with the stones of Benjamin and Lucy Rogers. Darrell Norris states "the close of the nineteenth century saw fewer Ontario gravestones decorated with motifs, owing to their comparatively low incidence on obelisks."[47] As suggested earlier, gravestones by the late nineteenth and early twentieth century were beginning to show a marked change in design. Accordingly some stones may have deliberately been left without a motif. In St. George's Cemetery , Pioneer Memorial Cemetery and Harbour Pioneer Cemetery a large percentage of stones have no motif present (50.3% , 42.6% and 39.1% respectively) clearly indicating the need for a category specific to the motif-less stones. The high numbers may lead one to the conclusion not having a motif was the most popular form of gravestone decoration or non-decoration. A walk through an early graveyard would support the idea the vast majority of stones had no motifs. However a number of factors may hinder an accurate accounting of stones with no motifs. In some cases wear and attrition have led to the motif becoming obliterated . In other instances partial stones have been mounted in a cairn (this was the case in the Pioneer, Farewell and Harbour Pioneer Cemeteries) and the upper portion of the stone where one expects the primary motif to be located is missing. It is important to note the stones placed in the motif- less category are cases where no motif was ever part of the stone. For cases where the presence of a motif cannot be established with certainty, a notation of undetermined would be used. These stones were not included in the study. Table 9 illustrates the frequency of motif-less stones in the cemeteries.

Table 9  Frequency of Motif-less Stones by Cemetery

| CEMETERY | Number of Stones (% of total in cemetery) |
| --- | --- |
| Farewell | 0 |
| Union | 0 |
| Pioneer | 58 (42.6) |
| Harbour | 9 (31.9) |
| St George's | 27 (50.9) |
| Total | 94 |

It is certainly feasible to assume not all stones were carved with a motif. Possibly the cost of having a stone inscribed with a design was prohibitive to many settlers. An invoice in the amount of $140.00 from the J.J. Wolfenden Stone Cutters and Monument Dealers in Whitby dated 1883 attests to the fact stones with an engraving may not have been in the budgets of the majority of settlers.[48] Burrell theorizes many of the stones in this category belong to children suggesting the extra cost of having a design engraved may not have been viewed as a worthwhile expenditure during this period of high infant mortality. Deaths may have come quite unexpectedly leading to a hasty erection of a monument which was intended to be replaced with a more permanent marker at a later date. However this theory does not prove to be true in the Oshawa examples where a disproportionate number of motif-less stones are actually from the graves of adults and not children. In St. George's Anglican Cemetery 20 stones from a possible 27 motif-less stones ( or 74% of the stones in the motif-less category) are adults and in the Pioneer Memorial Cemetery the numbers are even more dramatic where 45 of 58 (or 77.5%) stones with no motif are adults.

The question that needs to be asked is what, if any, correlation exists between the economic and social standing of an individual and the motif, or lack thereof, on the gravestone. David Burrell, in his study of Geauga County, Ohio has suggested there are difficulties with assuming economics was a major contributing factor to gravestone design.[49] The stone of Elder Thomas Henry and his wife Lurenda (1879) in the Harbour Pioneer Cemetery (see above) may offer some insight for choosing a marker without iconography. Considered to be a moderately wealthy man, Elder Henry was a minister in the Christian Church and respected as a pious man working to spread the gospel. Although his stone is not of the slab variety it is a simple monument which does not display any iconography and only a short epitaph . The message is simplicity and seems befitting for a man who lived a simple life centered on church and his family. There is little doubt the family could have afforded a much more elaborately decorated monument and professional carvers were in the area at the time of his death. However one can speculate this simple marker was chosen deliberately to convey a way of life enjoyed by the deceased.

Burrell notes that 40% of stones between 1800-1821 and 57% between 1822-1825 in Geauga County lack iconography .[50] Although the test sample is relatively small these figures do compare with the numbers of motif-less stones in Oshawa. Burrell theorizes the lack of iconography on gravestones may in fact be related to a serious devaluation of religious spirit.[51] The argument for the classical revival motifs indicating a corresponding lack of spirituality in the population can be used here as well. Possibly stones sans motif are an indication of departure from the depiction of religious themes. During the latter part of the nineteenth century an increasingly secular image of death began to prevail which was marked by unconventional symbols of death and faith.[52] This may have in turn led to increasing preference for no iconography to adorn gravestones.

# The Cemeteries

*The founders of a new colony, whatever Utopia of human virtue and happiness they might originally project, have invariably recognized it among their earliest practical necessities to allot a portion of the virgin soil as a cemetery, and another portion as the site of a prison."*

~ Nathanial Hawthorne

The five cemeteries chosen for this study are the oldest burial grounds in Oshawa with the majority of their burials predating 1900 . Each graveyard represents a particular type of burial ground and therefore comprises a cross representation of the available resources. Harbour Pioneer Cemetery and Pioneer Memorial Cemetery, represent the two oldest cemeteries in Oshawa. St. George's Anglican and Pioneer Memorial are church burial grounds although the churches have long since moved premises. Farewell Cemetery is a private family burial ground and Union Cemetery, on the border of Oshawa and Whitby, is the largest cemetery in Oshawa at over 30 acres and 25 000 burial sites. A brief historical overview is presented for each cemetery followed by a discussion of the classification system in relation to each cemetery. Specific iconographic trends for each cemetery will also be identified.

*An early photo of the Harbour Pioneer Cemetery prior to its removal to a location on Bonnie Brae Point.*

# Farewell Cemetery

*Sweet little one, calm be thy sleep, Another's tears bedeck thy brow, Sisters and brothers around thee weep, A father's heart is asking how.*

*~ Julia Wright, epitaph*

Acheus Moody Farewell Sr. placed the following advertisement in the Oshawa *Vindicator* in 1866:

> ## Harmony Burying Ground.
>
> A FEW PLOTS in the above burial ground may be had by applying to the subscriber.
>
>         **A. M. FAREWELL, Senr.**
>
> Harmony, March 28, 1866.     43w4

The Harmony Burial ground was a 25m by 75m tract of land on the southeast corner of Harmony Road and Highway 2 (Lot 12 Harmony Plan) originally donated by A. Moody Farewell Sr. to be used as a private burial ground for Farewell friends and family. Each of Moody Farewell's 6 surviving sons received a portion of the burial ground for their families. Members of the Hinkson and Brown families were also given permission to be buried there.

In 1956 the City of Oshawa became the owner of the cemetery with a conveyance signed by heirs of Calston Horn who died in 1943. Horn was deeded the land in 1874 and the cemetery was part of his estate. By 1955 a provincial inspector reported the cemetery was in an abandoned state and by 1968 it was closed to further burials. The City of Oshawa secured funds to construct a memorial cairn to showcase the headstones and upgrade the grounds to pay homage to some of Oshawa's earliest settlers buried here. The official dedication took place on September 20, 1979.

*Interment in this cemetery took place*

*between 1815 and 1941 . . .*

*At this site are interred some of Oshawa's earliest settlers, and is truly an historical landmark*

The Farewell Cemetery made news again in 1993 when the Region of Durham decided to widen Harmony Road. Engineering studies indicated that as many as 38 graves were located outside the boundaries of the cemetery, encroaching 8.5 meters onto the road allowance.

Before any road work could commence, the cemetery had to be proclaimed an "unapproved cemetery" by the Provincial Registrar of Cemeteries. This occurred in July 1993, permitting the Region to proceed with the relocation of the human remains. The Toronto firm of Archaeological Services Inc. (ASI) was engaged to excavate, remove and rebury the remains. The excavation uncovered a total of 38 skeletons or partial skeletons in the road allowance.

*Recent photo of Farewell Cemetery, Oshawa. Photo by Melissa Cole*

ASI removed the remains for a short period of osteological analysis and reburied the physical remains along with any personal effects, in concrete vaults within the property line of the cemetery. A large array of coffin hardware including handles, viewing glass and hinges, were recovered from the excavation and this collection was placed in the Oshawa Community Museum.

There are 52 stones in the cemetery many of which are fragments located in a cairn, therefore only 22 or 42.3% of the total stones fit the established criteria and were able to used in this study. Transcription records from the Oshawa/Whitby Chapter of the Ontario Genealogical Society completed between 1970-1975 were used to decipher details on many of the stones.

Farewell Cemetery represented the smallest sample used however all the stones were easily categorized with the classification system. Table 10 illustrates the vast majority of stones (72.7%) have either a floral or classical revival style motif. The nine floral stones comprised five women and four children. Classical revival expressions included willows in all seven examples and urns in four. The dates for classical revival motifs ranged from the 1830s to the 1860s with the majority appearing in the 1850's.

Table 10  Frequency of Motif Types in Farewell Cemetery

| Motif | Number of Stones (% of total in cemetery) |
|---|---|
| Floral | 9 (40.9) |
| Classical Revival | 7 (31.8) |
| Hand | 3 (13.6) |
| Animal | 2 (9) |
| Figure | 1 (4.5) |
| Motif-less | 0 |
| Miscellaneous | 0 |
| Total | 22 |

## Abram Farewell

The fifth child of Acheus Moody Farewell and Elizabeth Annis, Abram Farewell was born on December 21, 1812 in the Village of Harmony. Abram attended a local school throughout his childhood earning a good, common education. His first position as an adult was as a schoolteacher in the Village of Harmony. It was during this time that he met Caroline Stone, 7th child of Benjamin and Catharine Stone, born March 10, 1812. The two were married on January 18, 1837 and together they had two children, Wilson Murton, born September 1847 and Franklin A., born September 1850. Both Wilson and Franklin passed away as young children, at the ages of 1 year and 3 months, respectively. Abram and Caroline later adopted 5-year-old John Edwin Kellogg (Farewell).

As an industrious fellow, Abram moved on from his career as a schoolteacher and went to work for his father's business, eventually leaving to open his own general store. Abram also found success as part owner of a grain transportation operation. Abram's keen interest in political affairs resulted in his election as Deputy Reeve in the township of Whitby in 1854, the first Deputy Reeve in that township. In 1871 he was elected to the Provincial Legislature, representing South Ontario as a Liberal. After leaving politics he joined the firm of Sifton, Ward and Company, working steadfastly to acquire a contract for a portion of the Canadian Pacific Railway. Abram Farewell was also actively involved in the Disciples Church and the temperance movement.

Caroline Stone passed away from heart disease on June 7, 1885. Abram Farewell lived another three years passing away on February 8, 1888 of Bright's disease (kidney disease). Both Caroline and Abram are buried in Farewell Cemetery, Harmony Road, Oshawa. John Edwin became a Crown Attorney and passed away on December 29, 1923 of uremia. He is buried in Union Cemetery.

# Union Cemetery

*"He is not dead he only sleeps, Affection o'er his memory weeps, His spirit rests not here"*

~Early epitaph, 1874

Oshawa Union Cemetery was established in 1875 by the Oshawa Union Cemetery Company on the site of an earlier burial ground. The land lying to the west of the Highway 2 entrance (corner of Thornton Rd. North and King Street West) was the location of a brick Presbyterian Church built in 1837, the original Presbyterian cemetery, a manse and a school. The church is thought to be the first non-wooden public building in Ontario County. [53] It was large, seating 500 people and was used for church and educational meetings. The earliest recorded burial is that of Alexander Armstrong interred in 1837. The Church was destroyed by fire sometime after 1863. As the community of Thornton's Corners continued to grow the early burial ground became inadequate and the company purchased the land surrounding it for a new burial ground for both Oshawa and Whitby. In 1922 the cemetery became the property of the town through the generosity of George McLaughlin who purchased the shares held by the Ontario Loan and Savings Company . He then presented the property to Oshawa and also secured the title deeds to the adjacent Presbyterian Cemetery.

"Often could be read there the name of the seaport in the old land from which the family had set sail and perhaps the township in which they had settled here. If one were sympathetic with "simple annals of the poor" an interesting half hour could always be spent in a country churchyard especially if the family names were known to you."

D.S. Hoig, Reminiscences and Recollections.

Union Cemetery was the largest cemetery used in the study with more than 25,000 burials. Many of Oshawa's pioneer are buried in this cemetery including the Gibbs brothers, Reverend Robert Thornton, Robert McLaughlin and Edward Skae. The cemetery is still open for burials and is the only one operated by the City of Oshawa. Due to the large number of burials, a selection of 83 stones was used from the north and south Presbyterian sections and sections A, B, C, D, E and F (see the map for more details).

# Map of Union Cemetery

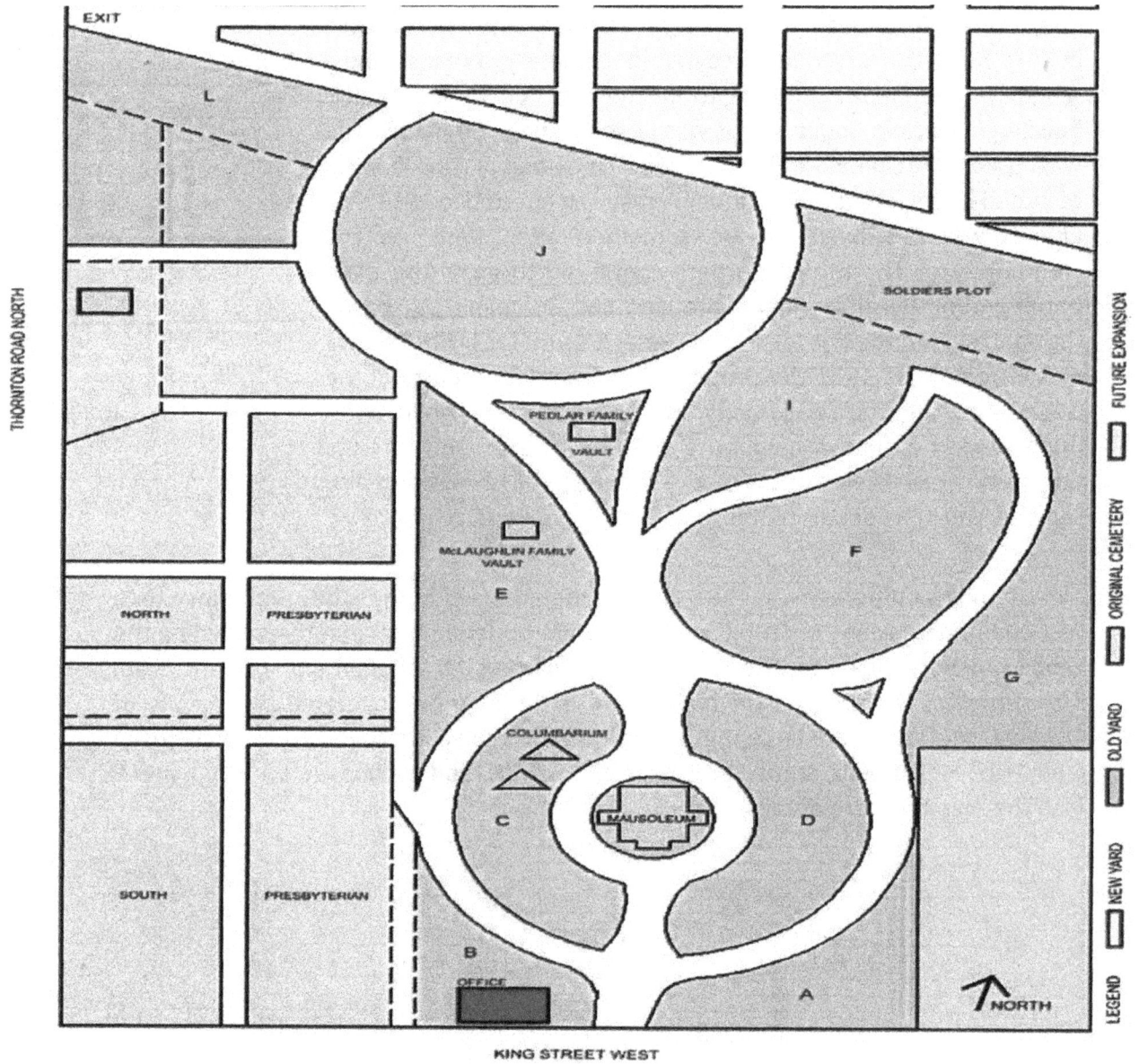

Transcription records completed by the Oshawa/Whitby branch of the Ontario Genealogical Society in 1983 were used to read the stones. The 83 stones were chosen from the oldest section of the cemetery because they fit the criteria as earlier established. Table 11 shows the breakdown of the motifs on the gravestones.

Table 11  Frequency of Motif Types in Union Cemetery

| Motif | Number of Stones (% of total) |
|---|---|
| Floral | 13 (15.6) |
| Classical Revival | 26 (31.3) |
| Hand | 31 (37.3) |
| Animal | 6 (7.2) |
| Figure | 0 |
| Motif-less | 0 |
| Miscellaneous | 7 (8.4) |
| Total | 83 |

The most popular motif was hands representing almost 40% of the motifs found in the cemetery. Although hand motifs spanned the years 1830-1890 the decades of the 1860s and 1870s had 22 examples representing 70.9% of the hand motifs reported. The most popular of the hand motifs was upwards pointing with 16 examples followed by clasping hands with 14 and downwards pointing with 1 example. Classical revival motifs spanned the period 1830-1880 with most appearing in the 1850s and 1860s consistent with results in other cemeteries. The largest percentage of miscellaneous motifs was found in the Union Cemetery. Such motifs accounted for 7 or 8.4% of the total. This was the largest sample of miscellaneous motifs in the cemeteries studied but hardly surprising given the large number of stones. Of the seven stones in the miscellaneous category, five were Masonic symbols all featuring the square and compass. Although the Masons had a strong presence in the Oshawa/Whitby area, the Union Cemetery was the only place where the Masonic symbols were found.

# Dr. Robert Thornton

Dr. Robert Hill Thornton was born in April 1806 in the Parish of West Calder near Edinburgh, Scotland. He was an ordained minister of the United Secession Church of Scotland and was sent to preach in Canada in 1833. Also in 1833 Dr. Thornton married Margaret Thompson. Dr. Kaiser states that Reverend Thornton and Margaret arrived in New York after a seven week journey and continued to Rochester where they arrived in time to celebrate the American Independence holiday on July 4. The Thornton's boarded a boat which they thought would bring them to Toronto but in fact was only going as far as Cobourg. Here Reverend Thornton left his wife while he traveled to find a home.

Reverend Thornton soon came upon a settlement of Scottish settlers in Whitby who asked him to become their minister. Reverend Thornton agreed upon the condition that he was allowed to continue his missionary work between Toronto and Cobourg. Thus Reverend Thornton became the first Presbyterian minister in the area.

The first meeting place of the Presbyterians was west of Union Cemetery on Moore's Hill in the township of Whitby. There stood a log building which was the Anabaptist Church as well as a place for political and town meetings. The first Presbyterian services in the district were held here. In 1837 the Presbyterians built their own church on the site which is now the Union Cemetery. The church was large and could seat 600 worshippers. Reverend Thornton continued to preach in this new location and raised funds to pay for the church with visits to the United States. In 1855 Reverend Thornton's heavy workload began to take a toll on his health and his parishioners raised $600 to send their minister and his wife to Scotland on a vacation.

In 1861 the Whitby and Oshawa sections of the Presbyterian Church separated and the Oshawa group constructed a church in 1862 at the corner of Simcoe and Bruce Streets. Several years later this church became too small and the present St. Andrew's Church was constructed in 1899.

Dr. Thornton also had a keen interest in education. He organized several schools between Toronto and Cobourg and also served as local Superintendent of Education and as an Inspector of Schools. He campaigned tirelessly as an advocate for temperance principles. Princeton University in New Jersey conferred the honour of LL.D. upon Reverend Thornton. Dr. Thornton died in 1875 and is buried in Union Cemetery.

# Harbour Pioneer Cemetery

*For few as were the living inhabitants of the township, this city of the dead was beginning to be built, and to gather in its dwellers.*

*From the Memoirs of Thomas Henry, 1880*

The earliest cemetery in Oshawa is the Harbour Pioneer Cemetery originally located east of the present day Port of Oshawa. Easily recognizable from Farewell Street South by the ring of trees surrounding it and the stone corner posts, the Harbour graveyard contained the remains of Oshawa's first settlers including Benjamin Wilson and members of the Guy, Henry and Robinson families. The earliest burial recorded on the gravestones was that of Nancy Henry, mother of Thomas Henry, who died in 1816. In *Memoirs of Thomas Henry*, Nancy's burial is mentioned, " she was buried with Christian rites, on the little hill by the lake". However it is possible burials may have occurred as early as 1800. The land on which the cemetery is located was initially part of a Crown grant to King's College and was later leased to Benjamin Wilson, the first settler in Oshawa. In 1904 the land was transferred to the first trustees Jackson Smith, John Robinson and Glen Henry. By the late 1960s there was talk of harbor expansion and the need for the cemetery to be removed to another location. Although there was a general feeling the cemetery should be kept intact, in 1973 Oshawa City Council decided to approve the removal of the cemetery to another location. A new location was found just west of the Oshawa Community Museum on the hill known as Bonnie Brae Point. In 1975 the remains of 195 persons and 62 gravestones were removed by Riverside Cemetery Company and placed in their new location on Bonnie Brae Point

"The choice of this bluff ensures that the waves of Lake Ontario will continue to sound a requiem to the early settlers and their progeny here interred."

From the total of 62 stones, it was determined 24, or 38.7% of the stones fit the criteria and could be included in the study. The other stones exhibited deterioration from weather and moss making it difficult to establish the existence of any motifs. Table 12 illustrates the breakdown of motif styles of the stones. The results indicate motif-less was the most popular category comprising 41.6% of the samples followed by floral and hands. The large number of stones in this sample lacking a motif deserve a closer look. Nine of the stones represent members from 4 of the most respected pioneer families of the Port area; 4 from the Henry, 3 from the Robinson, 1 from the Wilson and 1 from the Guy families. The tenth belongs to a child. With the exception of the child's stone (1851), all were carved and erected at a time when it is known professional stone carving was available in the area. The majority of the stones date from the period 1870-1880 which correlates with Burrell's theory of a preference for motif-less stones during this era of increasing devaluation of religion. However family histories indicate at least two of the families, namely the Henrys and the Robinsons were pillars of the religious community. It therefore does not appear a decline in religious expression played any particular part in the choice of a motif-less stone. It is possible a belief in simplicity and an aversion to showing off were the motivating factors in these examples.

# Thomas Guy Jr.

Thomas Guy Jr., was born in St. Gorran, Cornwall, England on March 21, 1819. Thomas Jr. married Harriet Cock in 1842 and they had two daughters, Harriet born in 1843 and Ellen in 1844. In 1846 following the lead of his parents and younger brother, Thomas Jr. immigrated to Canada with his family, his mother-in-law Harriet Cock Sr., her male servant and his wife. Thomas Jr. and his family settled on Reach Road where their third child, William Billing Guy, was born in 1847. In 1848 Thomas' wife Harriet died of typhoid. Thomas Jr. traveled to Woodstock with his brother James Odgers in 1850 eventually moving back to Oshawa in 1851 and settling on Sydenham farm just west of Port Oshawa on Bonnie Brae Point (formerly Guy's Point).

An 1871 notice placed in the Ontario Reformer advertised for sale the Sydenham farm. Described as "one of the best farms in the County of Ontario" Sydenham farm compromised 200 acres (of which 140 were under plough), 200 fruit trees and a frame house with a verandah. Thomas was a champion breeder and exhibitor of Ayrshire cattle, Shorthorn cattle, Leicester sheep and Berkshire pigs. He was best known for his Ayrshires winning numerous prizes at the local, provincial and national levels. In 1882 the Farmer's Advocate prize of $100.00 for best five cows at the Provincial Exhibition was won by Ayrshires owned by Thomas Jr.

In 1853 Thomas Jr. married Eliza Henry, the first child born to Lurenda and Elder Thomas Henry, and they had 5 children of their own, Eliza, Alford C., George, Frank T., and Emma. In December 1867 Eliza Henry Guy died of typhoid and was buried in the Harbour Cemetery. In that same year Thomas Jr.'s first born daughter Harriet also died of typhoid in Bowmanville and was buried in the Harbour Cemetery.

Thomas Jr. remarried for the third time in 1869. With this wife Hannah Every, he had three more children, Thomas, Kirby and Petronella. Hannah died in 1879 and Thomas Jr. remarried for the last time to Flora Douglas and they have one son, James Douglas Guy.

It appears Thomas Jr. never sold Sydenham farm for he died there in his 79th year on June 16, 1897. He was laid to rest in the Union Cemetery. After Thomas' death Flora and her son moved to Idaho in 1909 where she died in 1912.

Table 12  Frequency of Motifs in Harbour Pioneer Cemetery

| Motif | Number of Stones (% of total) |
|---|---|
| Floral | 5 (21.7) |
| Classical Revival | 2 (8.6) |
| Hand | 4 (17.3) |
| Animal | 3 (13) |
| Figure | 0 |
| Motif-less | 10 (41.6) |
| Miscellaneous | 0 |
| Total | 24 |

*An early image of Harbour Pioneer Cemetery prior to its removal to Bonnie Brae Point. Courtesy of the Oshawa Community Museum*

*Harbour Pioneer Cemetery today, Bonnie Brae Point*

# St. George's Anglican Cemetery

*A faithful friend and husband dear/ Tender parent neath here/ Great is the loss we here sustain/ We hope in heaven to meet again."*

~ Epitaph of Maurice Morris, 1879

In 1864 John Shier surveyed 1 ¾ acres of land on the eastern side of Park Road North for the purpose of a burial ground for the congregation of St. George's Anglican Church. At the time the cemetery was located on the western most boundary of the Village of Oshawa. The cemetery was officially sanctioned in 1864 however burials may have taken place much earlier than this date would suggest. In 1895 two parishioners, T.H. Carswell and Mr. Cowan, used parish records and record books from an early caretaker to record all the gravestone inscriptions. They note the first officially recorded burial took place in 1857 but the gravestones list 40 burials which predate 1864 with the earliest being 1841. Possibly the cemetery was used as a burial ground prior to its acquisition by the Bishop. Well known family names from Oshawa's history are represented in the cemetery including members of the Warren, Mothersill, Welch and Hyland families. Today the cemetery appears to be quite a distance from St. George's Memorial Church but archival records indicate the first location of the church was on the northeast corner of King Street and Park Road in 1848. The cemetery would have been located in close proximity to the church immediately north on Park Road. By 1858 the congregation had moved to a new church closer to the centre of town on the northeast corner of Centre and John Streets. The cemetery is still open for interments and is maintained by the Oshawa Golf Club and the cemetery board of St. George's Memorial Church.

*Bargain and sale, 21st November, 1864, John B. Warren and wife to the Right Reverend John Strahan, Lord Bishop of Toronto....Upon trust to hold the same forever for the purpose of a church yard and burial ground for the congregation of St. George's Church, Oshawa."*

Presently St. George's contains 140 stones many of which exist as fragments or are indecipherable. Therefore only 53 or 37.8% fit into the established criteria (Table 13). As this particular cemetery was the only example closely aligned with a church it provided a good opportunity to test the classification system in a setting where it is expected motifs may exhibit religious themes not seen in the other examples. However any religious symbols were able to be accommodated in the categories as predominate or secondary motifs. The sole example of a religious theme was the divine effigy of an angel portrayed on a single stone. Of the 53 stones, 27 or 50.9% exhibit no iconography at all whether due to deterioration or as a chosen motif style. Interestingly floral and animal motifs (22.6% and 13.2% respectively) were the two most prevalent motif styles. The motifs hands, classical revival and figures appear on one stone each (1.8%).

In comparison to the other cemeteries studied the lack of classical revival motifs in St. George's Cemetery deserves some discussion. Two willow trees appear on stones in

# Silas Fairbanks

*Silas Fairbanks was born in York (Toronto) on January 1st, 1821, the eldest son of Levi Fairbanks. After graduating from Upper Canada College , he studied law. At the age of 20, he moved to Oshawa and established his own law practice. He was appointed clerk of Divisional Court and he held that position for 9 years until 1850. On January 26, 1850, he was elected to the council at the first meeting held by the Village of Oshawa. He remained a member of council until 1856 when he was elected Reeve of Oshawa.*

*In 1851 he married Hannah Arkland, daughter of Charles Arkland.  In 1852, Silas and Hannah were blessed with a daughter Mary Louise, who later married Frank Egerton Gibbs, son of the Hoourable T. N. Gibbs. In 1854 the Fairbanks family had a daughter Kate, who became the organist at St. George's Anglican Church. A son was born to the couple in 1860.*

*In 1857, Silas was elected a Grammar School Trustee and served in that capacity until 1871. It was during this time that his parish church (St. George's) moved to the corner of Centre and John Streets. Fairbanks was a great influence in this move and was also one of the founders of the Sunday school at St. George's.*

SILAS B. FAIRBANKS

*He was initiated into St. John's Lodge #75(Toronto) on June 6th, 1859, passed July 11, 1859 and raised Aug. 8, 1859.          On July 20, 1860, Silas Fairbanks was named the first Worshipful Master U.D for Lebanon Lodge. In 1861, Lebanon Lodge #139 received its warrant of Constitution with Silas B. Fairbanks as Worshipful Master. In the following year (1862) he was re-elected Reeve of Oshawa.*

*In 1866  Fairbanks was again elected Reeve and re-elected to the School Board. 1866 was also the year that Silas Fairbanks and William McCabe, both members of Lebanon formed Pentalpha Chapter Lodge.     Fairbanks received his appointment to Grand Lodge in 1866 and on Feb. 12, 1867 he was presented with his Grand Lodge Regalia in Lebanon Lodge. 1867 saw him become 1st Principal of Pentalpha Chapter.*

*Silas died on August 15, 1871, at the age of 50.  Oshawa closed down for the day of his funeral; recorded as the largest ever held in the Town. He was buried in  St. George's Cemetery on Park Road N. Of the funeral a Whitby paper said, "The Lambskin and evergreens were dropped on the coffin and the last offices of honour and fraternal love were performed at the grave. Col. S. B. Fairbanks, a true man, and a good Mason, who we hope will find as he did in the Lodges here below; a worthy place in the Grand Lodge above, with the Great Architect of the Universe."*

the cemetery one dating to 1860 and the other was not included in the sample due to its lack of date. To have only two representative classical revival stones in a nineteenth century cemetery of 140 stones is curious. However when one takes into account the cemetery was officially established in 1864 at the tail end of the classical revival popularity it is not surprising there is a lack of classically inspired designs appearing. As mentioned previously classical revival motifs may have signified a decrease in religiosity of the public. This may have had a bearing in St George's as one of the denominational cemeteries represented in the study. Perhaps there was a covert preference by the congregation for motifs with a more religious persuasion, in particular "softer" symbols relating to animals and flowers.

Table 13  Frequency of Motif Styles in Harbour Pioneer Cemetery

| Motif | Number of Stones (% of total) |
|---|---|
| Floral | 12 (22.6) |
| Classical Revival | 1 (1.8) |
| Hand | 1 (1.8) |
| Animal | 7 (13.2) |
| Figure | 1 (1.8) |
| Motif-less | 27 (50.9) |
| Miscellaneous | 4 (7.5) |
| Total | 53 |

# Pioneer Memorial Cemetery

*"To heaven I hope my wife has gone/ To her in time I hope to come/In peace she lived, in peace she died/Life was desired but God denied."*

~ Epitaph of Elizabeth Willcock, 1865

The Pioneer Memorial Cemetery on Bond Street West is located on land originally owned by Mr. J.B. Warren and in 1847 sold to the trustees of the Wesleyan Methodist Church. The property was immediately east of the Anglican Church, with their cemetery located on the northern portion of the land (Park Road Cemetery). At the time of sale a portion of the land was set aside and designated as a cemetery although burials had occurred here for many years prior. The earliest burial recorded was Sabine Dearbourn, wife of Samuel Dearbourn in 1830. In 1868 the congregation of the church moved to their new facility on Simcoe Street South after which there were few burials in the cemetery. The last burial recorded was that of Barbara Hurd in 1906. Many of the burials were for the well to do members of the Town with large family plots separated by wrought iron fences two feet high and decorative posts connected by chains. By 1895 the old Wesleyan Church had been removed and the basement filled in. A picket fence protected the burial plots from the many grazing cattle in the area. By 1945 the families of those interred had for the most part removed the remains to plots in Union Cemetery leaving behind the gravestones. In 1949 a plan was finalized to clean up the cemetery property and install the stones in a series of cairns arranged in the shape of a six pointed star.

> *"Erected in 1949 by the Simcoe Street United Church in memory of those whose names are inscribed hereon and of others, not so recorded, who also sleep here."*
> *Memorial plaque on cairn*

*Front gates at Pioneer Memorial Cemetery.*

*Photo by Robert Bell*

Today the site is a public park dominated by the remnants of 146 gravestones arranged in the cairns many of which are complete or at least feature the upper portion of the stone. Of the 146 remaining stones, 93% or 136 were used in this study, the largest number of any cemetery. Many of the stones (39 or 28.6%) list death dates prior to 1850 and seven are from the decade 1810- 1819. There is always the possibility the very earliest stones were carved at a later date and backdated however the simple style, lack of adornments and crudely carved lettering probably suggest the stones were completed at the time, or shortly thereafter the time of death. The majority of the stones (92 or 67.6%) date from the period 1850-1860, a time when gravestones were becoming more highly decorated. Table 14 shows the breakdown of motif styles for the cemetery.

Table 14 Frequency of Motif Styles in Pioneer Memorial Cemetery

| Motif | Number of Stones (% of total) |
|---|---|
| Floral | 24 (17.6) |
| Classical Revival | 29 (21.3) |
| Hand | 13 (9.5) |
| Animal | 8 (5.8) |
| Figure | 2 (1.5) |
| Motif-less | 58 (42.6) |
| Miscellaneous | 2 (1.49) |
| Total | 136 |

Stones with no motif account for the largest category with 58 examples or 42.6% of the sample. Some of this large sample may be due to the very early death dates listed on several stones. Possibly the large number of motif-less stones may relate to the theory stones may have been erected hastily at the time of death with the hopes of providing a more substantial stone at a later date. An early history of the cemetery indicates many families removed their relatives to the Union Cemetery late in the nineteenth century and the cemetery was almost empty . Possibly at this time new gravestones were erected which could very well feature motifs. A future course of research could involve cross referencing the names from the Pioneer Cemetery with the burials at Union Cemetery to see if this was the case.

# William and Margaret Garfat

*William Garfat was born in Yorkshire England in 1792 and married Margaret Taylor in 1816. The Garfats arrived in Canada in 1832 from England with their three sons Francis (born 1818), John (born 1819) and William (born 1822). The family eventually settled in Port Oshawa about 1835 on land that belonged to the Annis family. Although Samuel Pedlar noted Garfat was a tailor by trade, he is listed as farming in Oshawa. The 1851 Agricultural Census shows William Garfat occupying 156 acres of BF Lots 14 and 15. He had 45 acres of crops including peas, potatoes, wheat and turnips and 76 acres for pasture. In 1838, daughter Hannah was born in Oshawa. Later it appears William and Margaret moved to Concession 2, Lot 13.*

*William Garfat, died on the 6th of March 1865, in his 73rd year. His wife followed the next year in 1866. They are both buried in the Pioneer Memorial Cemetery. The tombstone reads, THIS STONE WAS ERECTED BY THE / MEMBERS OF HIS CLASS IN GRATEFUL/ REMEMBRANCE OF HIS MANY VIRTUES/ AND OF THE ANXIOUS SOLICITUDE WITH/ WHICH HE WATCHED OVER THEIR SPIRITUAL/ AND ETERNAL INTERESTS.*

# Conclusions

*The cemetery is an open space among the ruins, covered in winter with
violets and daisies. It might make one in love with death, to think that
one should be buried in so sweet a place.*

~ Percy Bysshe Shelley

Early Ontario gravestones are windows into the past. Not only do they provide biographical data pertaining to the deceased, they are also a form of artistic and cultural expression. This expression is reflected on the stones by the motifs and illustrates contemporary attitudes and ideas towards life, death and the hope for everlasting life in the hereafter. As societal and religious views changed throughout the nineteenth century, so too did motif styles and preferences. Gravestone motifs should no longer be considered merely decorative ornaments but rather hallmarks of ideas. Therefore it is imperative a system for preserving, retaining and disseminating this information is developed prior to the complete destruction of this resource.

In the past there has been great reluctance on the part of researchers to record the motifs. Reasons for this range from the idea there are just too many design expressions to consider to a lack of knowledge and appreciation for the importance of this aspect of historical research. Previous attempts to develop a method for organizing motifs have failed because in the end they were too narrowly defined or simply unable to encompass the broad spectrum of meanings associated with the designs. Carole Hanks was the first, in 1974, to suggest a classification system for Ontario gravestone motifs based on their design elements.

With some revision, Hanks' ideas can be used to develop a province wide classification system for gravestone motifs. The classification system put forth in these pages for nineteenth century Ontario gravestone motifs is the result of utilizing Hanks' ideas to narrow a seemingly endless array of motifs into generic categories representing meaning and in some cases, design elements. The revisions made to Hanks' original classification system are designed to more accurately categorize motifs and their variations according to meaning and/or design. Hanks' categories "flowers" and "angels" were changed to "floral" and "figures" respectively to more accurately describe the design expressions appearing in Ontario's cemeteries. Floral would now include wreaths, garlands and thistles as well as flowers. Figures will include all figures both human and divine. Another category "none" or "motif-less" was added to accommodate stones which by design had no motif.

Revisioning Hanks' system resulted in seven categories of motifs, Hands, Figures, Classical Revival, Floral, Animals, None and Miscellaneous. These categories were then used as a basis for the *Nineteenth Century Ontario Gravestone Inventory Worksheet* included in the Appendix . Although several inventory methods are currently in use in the Province, this *Nineteenth Century Ontario Gravestone Inventory* Worksheet I believe, represents the first standardized approach for introducing a province wide classification system and a common inventory method. Such a system offers infinite possibilities for regional or provincial comparison studies which under the current system is near impossible. By utilizing common terms and language for the process of recording gravestones and in particular the motifs, comparisons between graveyards in cities, regions and even provincially will be possible.

In order to test the viability of this classification system, the seven categories were used in a field situation similar to that faced by researchers. Over 300 stones in five early cemeteries in Oshawa were classified using the system with impressive results. Although the studied sample is relatively small, several cemetery studies from both Ontario and the East coast were also utilized to test the viability of the system outside of Oshawa.

In the case of all 318 stones it was relatively easy to assign one of the seven categories to the motif. As noted earlier one of the failings of the Konrad/Norris classification system was the large number of motifs placed into the miscellaneous category. One of the outcomes of developing a new classification system was to ensure the vast majority of the motifs could be placed within a specific category thus eliminating the need (or at least most of the need) for a "catchall" category. In this classification system the miscellaneous category is reserved for specific motifs, in particular those relating to occupation or affiliation and complex expressions as defined. This goal was realized with only 13 or 4.1% of the 318 stones designated to the miscellaneous category as opposed to a minimum of 10% of stones classified as "other" in the Norris system.

Another failing of Norris' system was the confusion encountered when deciding which category a particular motif belonged, a result of too narrowly defining many motif styles. The system outlined herein utilizes meaning, and in some cases design, to define categories. Norris developed categories which arguably are related in meaning and should therefore be considered a single category particularly in the case of hands and classical revival motifs. When considering hand motifs Norris used two categories; the Hand of God and clasping to classify hand expressions. More specifically hands has four expressions on Ontario gravestones; upwards pointing, downwards pointing (Hand of God), presenting and clasping, all representing a type of relationship (usually) between the living and the dead. This common relationship meaning is the reason all four of the expressions are treated as a single category however with four styles. It was this same idea of a common meaning which lead to a single category to embrace the classical revival elements as opposed to the three separate categories preferred by Norris.

From personal experience in the field and discussions with other gravestone researchers in order to be successfully applied, the *Nineteenth Century Ontario Gravestone Inventory* Worksheet along with the classification system must be simple and easy to follow particularly for those with limited knowledge of gravestones. The Summary Sheet as prepared contains the information necessary for completion of the *Nineteenth Century Ontario Gravestone Inventory* Worksheet.    This summary can be utilized in the field until one becomes familiar with the system and where particular motifs are to be placed.    The categories themselves are designed to either be simply checked off as in the case of motif-less or given a one or two word response.    For example in "classical revival" terms such as urn, obelisk or willow tree would be used.    In the section marked inscription (on the reverse) more detailed information accompanied by a sketch or photo would be included.    "Undetermined" would be used in situations where it is impossible to conclude if a motif was present due to damage to the stone or missing pieces. Information regarding secondary motifs would also be collected utilizing the same terminology as for the primary motif.

The most popular motifs in descending order are Motif-less, Classical Revival, Floral, Hands, Animals, Miscellaneous and Figures.

Table 15  Overall Popularity of Motif Styles

| Motif | Number of Stones (% of total) |
|---|---|
| Motif-less | 94 (29.6) |
| Classical Revival | 65 (20.5) |
| Floral | 63 (19.8) |
| Hands | 52 (16.4) |
| Animals | 26 (8.2) |
| Miscellaneous | 13 (4.1) |
| Figures | 4 (1.2) |
| Total | 318 |

As seen in the Appendix, the    breakdown by decade shows there are several trends emerging for motif preference throughout the nineteenth century. Most notable is the consistency of the motif-less category throughout the nineteenth century as one of the most popular styles.  These results clearly indicate the importance of including motif-less as a category on its own merit.    A total of 94 stones representing nearly 30% of the sample were included in the motif-less category suggesting the idea of a motif-less stone was a legitimate choice for many people.    Various reasons were discussed to account for this trend, however suffice it here to say as a category motif-less continued its popularity throughout the century. Classical Revival motifs on the other hand enjoyed immense popularity during the decades of the 1840s, 1850s and 1860s accounting for 57 stones (28.5%). The first example of a classical motif was seen during the 1810s, however it is quite possible this early example was back dated. No examples were seen during the 1890s. These findings are similar to those of Konrad and Norris who reported the 1840s and 1850s as the most active in their study for classical revival designs. Of all the motif categories, classical revival is most closely linked to a popular trend or fad. The public appetite for Greek inspired designs in architecture and furniture styles is played out in the graveyards as well with classical designs such as urns, willow trees and obelisks appearing with great frequency on stones. As popular culture embraced this trend the appearance of such motifs begins to dominate gravestones during the middle part of the century. As with all fads interest soon wanes and again this is seen in the graveyards with classical revival motifs all but disappearing by the end of the century. When questioned, modern monument makers cannot recall ever using a classical revival design on a stone.

Apart from the very earliest part of the century, floral motifs appeared throughout the century. In the period 1850 through the 1860s floral motifs were seen in 42 examples (26% of total 161 stones). It should be noted these figures represent the stones on which floral was the primary motif. If one were to include the stones where floral appeared as a secondary motif, floral would be considered the most popular motif style during the nineteenth century. This popularity continues today as floral remains the most commonly chosen motif.

Hands was another example of a motif with longevity appearing in each decade after the 1820s. The peak period for hands was during the 1860s when it came in third behind classical revival and floral motifs, however as a motif hands continued to appear regularly throughout the century. Patterson notes hands was the most numerous and longest lasting of the motif styles in her study. The results from Oshawa appear to be more closely associated with Konrad and Norris' findings of hands occurring with steady frequency from 1840 throughout the century.

Ludwig, Burrell and Deetz and Dethlefsen argue for the emergence of an increasing secularization of gravestone motifs, beginning in the late eighteenth century, resulting in religious images being gradually replaced by secular or non-religious expressions. As discussed earlier, Deetz and Dethlefsen and Ludwig believe the shift away from the death's head common on eighteenth century stones to a softer more cherub appearance parallels a shift in religious views. Society's move away from the strict religious expressions of the Puritans was evident by the appearance on the gravestones of depersonalized designs representing secular images. These changes were explained by Deetz and Dethlefsen by the decline in the strictness of the Orthodox Puritans in the late eighteenth century. As the decline intensified gravestones began to exhibit more ethereal designs such as cherubs and later willow/urn motifs. As society moved further away from strict religious views, the more secularized and depersonalized gravestone motifs became. The shift culminated with the classical revival designs of willow trees, urns and obelisks, all images viewed more romantically than religiously. The increasing use of cherubs and classical revival images indicate people focused more on the romantic idea of an everlasting life in the hereafter with loved ones rather than on death itself.

Norris argues for a similar trend occurring in Ontario, although 100 years later. The shift can be described as more subtle not having the death's head transformation as an indicator but rather the appearance of classical revival motifs which signaled the beginning of the shift away from religious themes. As the nineteenth century drew to a close, floral and clasping hand motifs began to dominate the graveyard landscape. Whether this indicates a shift in society's sense of spirituality is highly speculative especially in view of the continual popularity of the "secular" categories, namely `none', `classical revival' and `floral', throughout the nineteenth century. This consistency lends weight to the idea that a shift may have been occurring but it was subtle to a point of being almost imperceptible. What is clear however is by the time large numbers of classical revival motifs began appearing, the predominance of secular images for motifs was virtually complete. If religious symbols did appear in the latter part of the century it was often in a softer, less obvert form, often represented with floral images. As discussed previously flowers had specific meanings often tied in with religion, however they were, and are, an intricate part of the mourning process. Today for the majority of the population the underlying meaning of specific types of flowers is forgotten, however floral continues to be the most popular choice as a gravestone motifs. Modern floral expressions are more likely related to the mourning process more so than the expression of a religious idea. The small size of the Oshawa sample and the difficulty in obtaining examples of motifs from the early part of the nineteenth century make it to difficult to determine the correlation, if any, between religion and motif. With further research a more definitive picture of the religious landscape and its relation to motif choice will emerge.

Canadian and more specifically, Ontario, cemetery research has consistently lagged behind that of the United States. Much of Ontario's gravestone research has been characterized by local genealogical and historical societies working in isolation. Sharing this data to develop regional and provincial perspectives into research topics related to carving traditions and the correlation between economic status and gravestone choice will shed light on the entire gravestone industry and provide researchers with the background necessary to study motifs more closely. The classification system and the *Nineteenth Century Ontario Gravestone Inventory* Wor*ksheet* provide the necessary tools, I believe, from which to begin study. Gravestones are in danger from environmental agents and human vandalism. It is therefore imperative organizations such as the Ontario Genealogical Society and local historical societies be impressed upon to systematically record motifs along with the biographical information when transcribing gravestones.

# Appendix

# NINETEENTH CENTURY GRAVESTONE INVENTORY SHEET

Graveyard: _____

Location: · _____

Section: _____  Row: _____  Reference #: _____

Date Recorded: _____ H: _____ W: _____ D: _____

Photo Taken: _____

Name on Stone: _____ Sex: M _____ F _____

Date of Death: _____ Age at Death: _____

Relationships: _____

Carver Identification: _____

Type of stone:

Tablet                                In Cairn:

Flat Tablet                           Other:

| **Primary Motif** | **Secondary Motif** |
|---|---|
| Floral: | Floral: _____ |
| Classical Revival: | _____ Other: |
| Hands: | |
| Animals: | **Remarks** (Include motif location): |
| Figures: | |
| Miscellaneous: | |

**Inscription (include shape of stone, information on motif)**

# SUMMARY SHEET FOR NINETEENTH CENTURY GRAVESTONE INVENTORY

This *Information Sheet* will aid you in filling out the information on the *Nineteenth Century Gravestone Inventory*.

1. **Floral:** In Ontario the most prevalent motif style. For the purpose of this inventory floral is considered a primary motif only when it is represented on the stone, otherwise consider it a secondary motif. Representations may include single flowers, bouquets, wreaths and trees.

2. **Classical Revival:** This category may include columns, urns, obelisks and willow trees.

3. **Hands:** There are four variations of the hand motif in Ontario cemeteries;
   **Upwards Pointing:** Most common of the hand manifestations.

   **Clasping Hands:** Hands linked or clasping as in a handshake.

   **Presenting Hands:** Hand holding an item, most commonly a Bible or flowers

   **Descending Hand:** Least common of the four variations. Hand pointing downwards either pointing or holding an item, most commonly a scroll.

4. **Animals:** Most often seen on stones of children. Common depictions include birds (doves in particular) and lambs.

5. **Figures:** There are two common representations of this motif, human and divine.
   **Human:** May include human mourning figures or representations of Adam and Eve. Does not include portrait stones.

   **Divine:** May include representations of angels or cherubs.

6. **Miscellaneous:** This category is reserved for motifs which do not fit into any other category. May include religious symbols (crosses), occupational symbols or affiliations. Include in this category complex motifs containing two or more motif categories.

7. **Motif-less:** This category is reserved for stones which never had a motif. Use **Undetermined** for stones with missing parts or undecipherable motifs.

# Cemetery Terminology

| Symbol/Term | Interpretation |
|---|---|
| **A.E.** | Short for *Aevum,* Latin for years of life |
| **Anchor** | Hope |
| **Angel** | Transports soul to heaven |
| **Animal** | Lambs/doves – purity, peace, devotion, youth<br><br>Often seen on stones of children |
| **Ark** | Passage through troubled times |
| **Classical Revival Motifs** | Examples include urns, columns and obelisks<br><br>Popularity of these designs linked to the interest in Greek and Roman archaeological finds during the late 18th and early 19th centuries. |
| **Consort** | A widower, was alive at time of wife's death |
| **Curtains** | Final act in life, curtain comes down |
| **Death Heads** | Winged skull designs on early colonial gravestones. Eventually evolved into winged angels, and cherubs.  Represent the soul's journey to heaven |
| **Flowers** | Lily/rose – purity<br><br>Foliage/fruit – lushness of heaven<br><br>Ivy – Christian constancy<br><br>Palms – peace, victory<br><br>Thistle – national flower of Scotland<br><br>Flower bud/broken bud – life cut short, budded on earth but will bloom in heaven |
| **Floral wreaths** | Mourning<br><br>Often used to frame an epitaph |
| **Footstone** | Smaller stones placed at the foot of the grave. May display initials or name of deceased. |
| **Hands** | Represent a relationship between living and dead<br><br>Upwards pointing – hope for deceased to travel heavenward<br><br>Linked hands – union, greeting with the hope of meeting a loved one again<br><br>Upwards presenting - usually holding a Bible or flowers<br><br>Descending hand – usually holds an object such as a scroll, |

| | |
|---|---|
| | symbolically the hand of God |
| **Headstone** | Grave markers which are upright tablets placed at the head of the grave |
| **IOOF** | Independent Order of Odd Fellows<br><br>Symbol is the three links of chain representing Friendship, Love and Truth. Other symbols may include a shepherd's crook, clasped hands and a bow and arrow. |
| **Maker's Mark** | If present, can usually be found in the lower left hand corner of the stone. May indicate where stone was carved and by whom. |
| *Memento Mori* | Latin for *Remember Death* |
| **Motif** | A design appearing on gravestones |
| **Primary Motif** | Motif located in centre of stone or largest motif |
| **Relict** | Widow, was alive at time of husband's death |
| **Secondary Motif** | Motif that functions as a decorative detail for primary motif. Often floral motifs will be classified as secondary |
| **Slab stone** | Grave markers placed flush against the ground |
| **Square and Compass** | Mason |
| **Tempus fugit** | Latin for "Time flies" |
| **Willow tree** | Symbol of longevity, gospel of Christ. Appears to "weep" representing the sorrow and grief of mourning |

# Popularity of Motifs By Decade 1800 -1899

## Popularity of Motifs 1800-1809

| Motif | Number of Stones (% of total in decade) |
|---|---|
| Floral | 0 |
| Classical Revival | 0 |
| Hands | 0 |
| Animal | 0 |
| Figure | 0 |
| Motif-less | 1 (100) |
| Miscellaneous | 0 |
| Total | 1 |

## Popularity of Motifs 1810-1819

| Motif | Number of Stones (% of total in cemetery) |
|---|---|
| Floral | 0 |
| Classical Revival | 1 (12.5) |
| Hands | 0 |
| Animal | 0 |
| Figure | 0 |
| Motif-less | 7 (87.5) |
| Miscellaneous | 0 |
| Total | 8 |

## Popularity of Motifs 1820-1829

| Motif | Number of Stones (% of total in decade) |
|---|---|
| Floral | 1 (50) |
| Classical Revival | 0 |
| Hands | 0 |
| Animal | 0 |
| Figure | 0 |
| Motif-less | 1 (50) |
| Miscellaneous | 0 |
| Total | 2 |

## Popularity of Motifs 1830-1839

| Motif | Number of Stones (% of total in cemetery) |
|---|---|
| Floral | 1 (11) |
| Classical Revival | 3 (33.3) |
| Hands | 1 (11) |
| Animal | 0 |
| Figure | 0 |
| Motif-less | 4 (44.4) |
| Miscellaneous | 0 |
| Total | 9 |

## Popularity Of Motifs 1840 -1849

| Motif | Number of Stones (% of total in decade) |
|---|---|
| Floral | 3 (7.6) |
| Classical Revival | 12 (30.7) |
| Hands | 2 (5) |
| Animal | 0 |
| Figure | 1 (2.5) |
| Motif-less | 20 (51.2) |
| Miscellaneous | 1 (2.5) |
| Total | 39 |

## Popularity of Motifs 1850-1859

| Motif | Number of Stones (% of total in decade) |
|---|---|
| Floral | 17 (20.9) |
| Classical Revival | 26 (32) |
| Hands | 5 (6.1) |
| Animal | 12 (14.8) |
| Figure | 2 (2.5) |
| Motif-less | 16 (19.7) |
| Miscellaneous | 3 (3.7) |
| Total | 81 |

## Popularity of Motifs 1860-1869

| Motif | Number of Stones (% of total in decade) |
|---|---|
| Floral | 25 (31.2) |
| Classical Revival | 19 (23.7) |
| Hands | 18 (22.5) |
| Animal | 9 (11.2) |
| Figure | 0 |
| Motif-less | 8 (10) |
| Miscellaneous | 2 (2.5) |
| Total | 80 |

## Popularity Of Motifs 1870-1879

| Motif | Number of Stones (% of total in decade) |
|---|---|
| Floral | 11 (22.4) |
| Classical Revival | 1 (2) |
| Hands | 6 (12.2) |
| Animal | 3 (6.1) |
| Figure | 1 (2) |
| Motif-less | 22 (44.8) |
| Miscellaneous | 5 (10.2) |
| Total | 49 |

## Popularity of Motifs  1880-1889

| Motif | Number of Stones (% of total in cemetery) |
|---|---|
| Floral | 8 (20.5) |
| Classical Revival | 3 (7.6) |
| Hands | 8 (20.5) |
| Animal | 3 (7.6) |
| Figure | 1 (2.5) |
| Motif-less | 11 (28.2) |
| Miscellaneous | 5 (12.8) |
| Total | 39 |

## Popularity of Motifs 1890-1899

| Motif | Number of Stones (% of total in cemetery) |
|---|---|
| Floral | 2 (20) |
| Classical Revival | 0 |
| Hands | 3 (30) |
| Animal | 0 |
| Figure | 0 |
| Motif-less | 4 (40) |
| Miscellaneous | 1 (10) |
| Total | 10 |

# Endnotes

[1] Tamara Anson-Cartwright, Landscapes of Memories: A Guide for Conserving Historic Cemeteries (Toronto: Ministry of Citizenship, Culture and Recreation, 1997), 6.

[2] Anson - Cartwright

[3] See www.e-laws.gov.on.ca/html/statutes/english/elaws_statutes_90o18_e.htm for the Ontario Heritage Act.

[4] Referring to the study of death and dying.

[5] Kenneth Jackson and Camilio Vergara, *Silent Cities* (New York: Princeton Architectural Press, 1989) 10.

[6] Roger Hall and Bruce Bowden, "Beautifying the Boneyard: The Changing Image of the Cemetery in Nineteenth Century Ontario," *Material History Bulletin 2* (1986): 14

[7] Anson-Cartwright, 8.

[8] See www.e-laws.gov.on.ca/html/statutes/english/elaws_statutes_90o18_e.htm for the Ontario Heritage Act.

[9] China Galland, Love Cemetery (HarperOne, 2008)

[10] Hanks, 10.

[11] Anson-Cartwright, 8.

[12] Emily Wasserman, *Gravestone Designs* (New York: Dover Publications Inc., 1972), 10.

[13] Edmund Gillon Jr., *Early New England Gravestone Rubbings* (New York: Dover Publications, 1966), xxii

[14] Anson- Cartwright, 228

[15] Oshawa Times, November 3, 1984

[16] Harriet Forbes, *Gravestones of New England,* (New York: Da Capo Press, 1967), 22.

[17] Darrell Norris, "Ontario Gravestones", *Markers 1* (1987): 123

[18] Wasserman, 10.

[19] Trask, 15.

[20] Forbes, 22.

[21] Allan Ludwig, *Graven Images* (Connecticut: Wesleyan University Press, 1966) 34.

[22] Ludwig, 69.

[23] Norris, 122-149

[24] Norris, 124

[25] Nancy-Lou Patterson, "United Above Though Parted Below: The Hand as a Symbol on Nineteenth Century Southwest Ontario Gravestones," *Markers VI* (1995): 182.

[26] Although Patterson used three categories of hand motifs for her study I have included a fourth, the downward pointing hand. The symbolic meaning of the downward pointing hand is sufficiently different enough, in my opinion, from the pointing hand to warrant a category of its own.

[27] Patterson, 185

[28] Patterson, 185

[29] Patterson, 185

[30] Trask, 32

[31] Jacobs, 26

[32] Theodore Feder, *Great Treasures of Pompeii and Herculaneum* (New York: Abbeville Press Inc., 1978), 7.

[33] Although trees and branches are evident on stones after the turn of the century, no willow trees were seen. A contemporary monument maker confirmed willow trees are not common on gravestones today.

[34] Stone and Russell, "Observations on Figures, Human and Divine on Nineteenth Century Ontario Gravestones," *Material History Bulletin 3* (1986): 24.

[35] Stone and Russell, 23.

[36] Trask, 15.

[37] Ludwig, 142

[38] Stone of Fanny Martilla Cook, 1 year old child who died in 1860. Pioneer Memorial Cemetery, Oshawa

[39] Hanks, 34.

[40] Hanks, 56.

[41] The stone in question is that of John Stephenson who died in 1854. The stone depicts a common rendition of a lamb laying beside a willow tree. Located in the Pioneer Memorial Cemetery.

[42] Laurel Gabel, "Rituals, Regalia and Remembrance: Fraternal Symbolism and Gravestones," *Markers XI* (1991):5

[43] George Every, *101 Years of Craft Masonry in the Town of Whitby* (Whitby: C.A. Goodfellow and Son, 1927), 3.

[44] Don Bower, former Master Port Perry Lodge, Personal Communication, 1996

[45] Leeanne Fitzgerald, "Independent Order of Oddfellows," *Historical Happenings 3* (Oshawa Historical Society, 1997):4

[46] Fitzgerald

[47] Norris, 124

[48] J.J. Wolfenden file, Whitby Archives

[49] Dave Burrell. Life in the Stones: Gravestones of Geauga County, Ohio, 1800-1825, www.historicalinsights.com/dave/life.html 1996. Accessed on August 15, 2012

[50] Burrell, pg 6.

[51] Burrell, pg. 7

[52] Burrell, pg. 7

Biographical data courtesy of the Oshawa Community Museum